Dream Book
Lucid Dreaming and Dream Recall

DREAM BOOK TRILOGY 1

CRAIG HAMILTON-PARKER

Life Is a Dream - Realize It!
Sathya Sai Baba.

Copyright © 2000 Craig Hamilton-Parker
Previously published as:
The Dream Handbook – Create Space ISBN 9781503004306
Remembering Your Dreams – 2000 Sterling Publishing ISBN 0-8069-4343-2
Unlock Your Secret Dreams – Sterling Publishing ISBN 1-4027-0316-3

All rights reserved.

ISBN-13: 978-1533299093

ISBN-10: 1533299099

CONTENTS

1. **What Are Dreams?** — 1
   Primitive and Tribal Dreams, Native American Dreamers, Aboriginal Dreamtime, Ancient Egyptians, Greeks and Romans, Dream Spaces, Recall Technique, Function of Dreams, Sigmund Freud, Carl Jung,

2. **The Art of Sleep** — 12
   Curing Insomnia, Herbal Aids, Dream Foods, Sleep Hormones, Preparing for Sleep, Larks and Owls, Sleep Techniques, Prana Breathing, 3 Nidra Breath Techniques, Relaxing, Deep Relaxation Experiment.

3. **Recall, Lucidity and Experimentation** — 24
   Interrupting Early Sleep Cycles, Late Sleep Cycles, Inner Attitude, Basic Dream Recall and Lucidity, Dream Diary, Sensory Recall, Sounds, Sensations, Recall Routines, Dream Notices, Streams of Consciousness, Working with Imagery, Ink Blot Technique, Externalizing your Dream, Invisible Friends, Doodle Techniques, Working with Mandalas, Dream Maps, Multiple Dream Recall, Dream Dictionary, I Ching Experiments, Tarot, Edgar Cayce, Cayce's Methods.

4. **Working with Your Dreams** — 66
   Dream Interpretations, Dream Symbols, Common Dreams, How to Interpret a Dream, Feelings, Content Overview, Dream Landscapes, Observation Techniques, Who is in your Dream? Observing Detail, Recurring Dreams, Putting Dreams to use, Technique to use Dreams to Solve Problems.

5. **Lucid Dream Techniques** — 78
   What are Lucid Dreams? Your Spiritual Double, Creating a Doppelgänger, Triggering Lucid Dreams, Reality Testing Techniques, Jumping and Flying, Dream Memory, Changing Reality, Improving Lucidity, REM Cycles and Lucid Dreaming, Getting up too early, Tibetan Dream Control, Cloud Walking, Learning to Fly, Lindbergh's Astral Flight, Out-of-Body Dreams, How to Astral Travel, Dream Body Perceptions, Opening the Third Eye, Third Eye Chakra Experiments, Shared Dream Memories, Meeting in Dreams,

6 **Remembering Past Lives**   99
Dream to Remember Past Incarnations, Remembering Lost Childhood Memories, The Past Lives of George S Patton, How to Remember you Birth, Dreamscapes, Childhood Dreamscapes, Symbolic Dreamscapes, Foreign Dreamscapes, Out-of-Body Dreamscapes, Celebrity Past Lives, Past Life Dreamscapes, Case Study: Shanti Devi, Past Life Recall for Self-Improvement, Recognizing People you Knew in your Last Incarnation, Group Souls, How Many Lives? Remembering Animal Past Lives,

7 **Seeing the Future**   117
How to See the Future, Theories about Premonition, Do you Dream of the Future? What is ESP? Psychic Test, Dreaming of the Future, Dream Incubation for Prophecy, Incubating Future Dreams, Prophecies you may have already made, How to Dream About the Future, The Dreaming Soul.

THE DREAM BOOK TRILOGY

This book is part of the *Dream Book Trilogy* . See the back pages for other books in this series. In book 2 you will learn to Interpret Dreams and Fantasies and in Book 3 you will learn to work with dream clairvoyance.

BECOME THE MASTER OF YOUR DREAMS

In this book Craig Hamilton-Parker shows you how achieve total dream recall and awaken the hidden powers of your dreams. Craig has appeared many times on television as a dream interpreter, hosted his own show 'Nightmares Decoded and is also well-known for his clairvoyant and mediumistic abilities. He is a best-selling author.

Using simple but powerful techniques you will first be shown how to remember your dreams with great clarity. You will then increase the intensity of your dreams and know how to make immediate and accurate interpretations of their meanings. Once you are attuned to your inner dream life, you will begin to become master of your unconscious and learn to control your dreams and use them like a biological computer to solve problems and increase your creativity.

Through a series of easy-to-understand exercises you will learn to become fully lucid in a dream. You will learn to control the dream as it is taking place and discover ways to access your hidden potential. You will awaken in the dream and take control of its contents like the director of a film. You will also learn techniques such as astral travel and how to project the spirit body during sleep.

As a final stage you will discover how to access your own clairvoyant abilities and trigger dreams that are maps of the potential future. You will discover amazing things about yourself and the incredible potential that you have locked away in your unconscious mind.

Master these techniques and your dreams will give you access to your past lives and insights into the future.

1 WHAT ARE DREAMS?

To sleep; perchance to dream; aye, there's the rub.
Shakespeare, *Hamlet*

Dreams were once considered visions of the highest order. Ancient man was more in touch with his inner self and the workings of the soul than we are today. He went to sleep firmly believing that when he awoke dreams would provide him messages from the gods. For him, dreams may have been easy to recall as they were considered an essential part of life and were highly valued.

In sleep we have the power, in a perfectly normal and natural way, to get valuable instruction and insight. In sleep we can connect with our soul life and discover that part of ourselves that relates to the infinite spirit. The majority of people in the modern world are unaware of this and do not have access to these tools.

Dreams also put us in touch with the dark side of ourselves, the unconscious, unrecognized aspects of our personality. By using dreams to discover this shadowy side, we can become more integrated, self-aware and more well-rounded individuals. A great many people are completely unaware of their own shortcomings and faults and will rarely criticize themselves. Instead of looking within to root out the weeds of ignorance they project their own faults onto others or blame circumstances. In particular, they attribute to other people all the evil and inferior qualities that they do not like to recognize in themselves. They criticize and attack these *bêtes noires*, making them the scapegoat for their own inferior qualities. Everything that is unconscious in themselves is projected onto their neighbor, and they treat them accordingly.

Primitive and tribal dreamers

Early societies made a similar premise to the point that there was little distinction between the inner and outer world. Dreams were considered reality, and people made very little separation between what happened in world and the psychological processes within. In the same way that many people today project their unconscious hopes and fears onto other people, so early man projected his inner processes onto the world. In short, no distinction was made between the world of dreams and real life.

Many of these beliefs continue in tribal societies today. For example, the Kai tribe of New Guinea and the West African Ashantis believe that if a man dreams of committing adultery, he must be tried and punished. The subject of the dream is also punished. At the trial, the witness is asked to recall his dream in detail. Accepting the reality of the dream, the accused will acknowledge the charge. In such societies, the events that happen in dreams have the same reality and are treated with the same gravity as a real-life crime.

Native American dreamers

Native American cultures held similar beliefs about the reality of dreams. For example, a Cherokee bitten by a snake in a dream would seek a healer's treatment for snakebite on awakening. Dreams shaped every aspect of Native American life. A dream was the soul's journey to another world, a way to receive spiritual instruction and guidance. Sometimes these visions contained personal content and at other times they pertain to the whole tribe.

Many Native American rituals, dances, songs, and paintings were received in dreams. Medicine men healers gained their power and inspiration from dreams. Dreams indicated the causes of illness and the individual's power to cure himself. They were also considered the way to maintain good fortune in most aspects of life. A great deal of attention was paid to dreams. Among some Native Americans, mother customarily asked children in the morning if they had dreamed; dreams were encouraged and acted on.

The dream rituals of the Native Americans and tribal societies encouraged the subconscious to make them remember a dream. (Some modern psychologists call this "pre-sleep planning.") Dances, songs, sand paintings, and rituals were held to encourage dreams of great power that could be used to guide the whole tribe. Sometimes this dream incubation method involved sleeping in a place of special spiritual significance. The Plains tribes, such as the Blackfoot, Cheyenne, and Crow believed that the most powerful sacred site was the top of a prominent mountain.

When the Native Americans were expelled from their traditional lands a spiritual crisis occurred in their society. Their visionary quests could not be held in the limited confines of the reservation. For them the land was not just for growing crops; the land had sacred spaces that nurtured the living soul of the tribe.

Aboriginal Dreamtime

Similarly the Aborigines of Australia lived out their dreams in the landscape around them. As with many other tribal societies, dreams were not something separate from waking life. The Aborigines based a large part of their rich culture around a state of consciousness called "Dreamtime." In this strange state of awareness they would wander the outback and be aware of spiritual states. There are stories and songs about these journeys. They have to do with the journeys of the ancestors and the "creation sites," places where different clans and animals were created. Others are about the precise route taken by an ancestor figure. During Dreamtime the past joins the present and future to become one.

According to tradition, Dreamtime originated thousands of years ago when the Aborigines first came to the shores of Australia from Asia. They gradually split into 500 territorially anchored groups and wandered the wilderness in a continual search for waterholes. Today when aborigines enter this state of consciousness they are connecting again to the knowledge and influence of their ancestors.

Aborigines enter this state through lucid dreams or by encouraging a sleeplike state while still awake. They appear detached from everyday existence. Once this hard-to-describe level of consciousness is attained they begin a journey that is both physical and spiritual at the same time. The traveler in Dreamtime goes beyond the world of what is generally accepted as reality and enters a new dimension of consciousness. He or she is able to communicate with the spirits of the ancestors and other spirits including those of nature. Dreamtime, signifies continuity of life unlimited by space and time. Only the old men and women had full knowledge of this and were given the authority in ritual and matters of social behavior.

Certain "dream elements" in the strange landscape of the Australian outback are important. Waterholes, markings on the landscape, hills, mountains, and the famous Ayres Rock are focal points where these Dreamtime forces are most powerful. The Aborigine will identify with these places of his ancestors from the time of creation and merge into this strange surreal world of awareness.

The Native American and Aboriginal dream traditions could be the echoes of far older traditions that stretch back to prehistoric times. Could it be that the megalithic sites such as Stonehenge, Avebury, and Carnac were also places where the world of dream and reality met? It is certainly likely that they were used for dream incubation.

My own feeling is that these sacred sites are where adepts of the magical arts would leave their bodies during sleep and travel to stars and other planes of existence. According to Celtic mythology the standing stones at Carnac are the place where the heroes rest on their journey to the Isles of the Blest. Could this perhaps be a symbol of the stepping-off point of the astral journey to the spiritual world that we could once access in dreams? Were Carnac, Stonehenge, and Glastonbury used for ritual re-enactments of a cosmic drama where, like the Aborigines, our ancestors could enter Dreamtime?

I believe that our prehistoric ancestors' Dreamtime was intricately linked to the geopathic forces found at the sites of standing stones, sacred wells and springs. Many people today feel the same eerie feeling when they visit these places. The ancient standing stones awaken something from the inner most depths of the unconscious. You can feel them tugging at the psyche encouraging us into the ancient world of Dreamtime.

The mysterious traditions ancient Egyptians

Many dream traditions similar to those of the early shaman can be found in diverse cultures from around the world. For example, the ancient Egyptians believed that certain places were conducive to the recall of dreams. They were one of the first societies to interpret the meaning of dreams and to develop oneiromancy, or dream divination.

An Egyptian text attributed to King Merikare, the pharaoh who ruled from about 2070 BC, tells us about the ruler's dreams and what they may foretell. He believed that dreams symbolized their exact opposite. For example, a disastrous dream foretells happiness, and happiness foretells disaster.

This tradition continued for centuries; one of the oldest records of dreams and their interpretations is a papyrus of 1250 BC, which records some 200 dreams and their meanings. The falcon-headed god Horus supposedly penned it.

The Egyptians believed that dreams contained messages from both good and evil spirits. To recall them and stimulate them, the Egyptians used many techniques including ingesting herbal potions, reciting spells, or sleeping in the temple. On awakening the dreamer would submit his or her dreams to the temple priest for interpretation.

In his book *A Search in Secret Egypt*, mystical writer Dr Paul Brunton explains how he discovered secret teachings that revealed that the Great Pyramid was once used as a place to dream. In the days before mass tourism he obtained permission from the Department of Antiquities to sleep in the King's Chamber.

Brunton had spent many years learning the art of meditation and slowly sank into a heightened state of awareness between sleep and waking. At first he saw "monstrous elemental creations, evil horrors of the underworld, forms of grotesque, insane, uncouth and fiendish aspect gathered around me with unimaginable repulsion," but these gave way to the figure of a priestly guide who revealed to him the secrets of the pyramid.

Brunton slipped into a "semi-somnolent condition" and was taken out of his body by the figure and into other worlds. The priest tells him:

"Know, my son, that in this ancient fane lies the lost record of the early races of man and the Covenant which they made with their Creator through the first if His great prophets. Know, too, that chosen men were brought here of old to be shown this Covenant that they might return to their fellows and keep the great secret alive. Take back with thee the warning that when men forsake their Creator and look on their fellows with hate, as with the princes of Atlantis in whose time this Pyramid was built, they were destroyed by the weight of their own iniquity, even as the people of Atlantis were destroyed."

(Students of American psychic Edgar Cayce, who was often called the "sleeping prophet," will note that Brunton's waking dreams revealed similar information about the link between the Great Pyramid of Gizeh and Atlantis. Indeed Brunton, like Cayce, claims that his dreams reveal the existence of secret chambers containing the lost knowledge from prehistoric civilizations.)

Brunton, like the Egyptians before him, was increasing the likelihood of recalling a dream by sleeping in a sacred place. A psychologist will tell you that these dreams were not stimulated or induced, instead that the psychological reinforcements of environment encouraged the dreamer to interrupt existing dream patterns. For example, if you tell yourself before going to sleep that you will have a dream, you increase the likelihood of immediately remembering a dream upon awakening. Sleeping in a special place that is said to make you dream will increase the subconscious programming to help you remember a dream when you wake up. The environment reinforces this pre-sleep planning. This technique is called "dream incubation" and will be discussed in detail in later chapters.

Many of the ancient dream rites were an early form of dream incubation. A favorite of the Egyptian priests was to draw a portrait of the god Besa in ink on the left hand. This was then wrapped in a black cloth. The ritual involved silently writing a petition to the god by the light of the setting sun. The ink was made from a magic potion that included the blood of white doves, frankincense, myrrh, cinnabar, rainwater, mulberry juice, and the juice of wormwood. This technique would ensure that the sleeper would remember the dream and that the dream would include a prophecy from the god.

Dreams of the Greeks and Romans

The ancient Greek civilization was greatly influenced by the Egyptians. The Greeks built more than three hundred temples and shrines that were used for dream incubation. They believed that if you slept in these temples the gods would answer questions or foretell the future with a dream. Dreams were the messages from the gods.

The sleeper would be visited by Hypnos, the god of sleep, who would fan them with the wings on his headdress. Hypnos was the brother of Thanatos, the god of death and the son of Nyx, the god of the night. He lived in the underworld, in the land of the Cimmerians, or in a cave on the island of Lemnos. Here, in this mysterious, dark and misty chamber ran the waters of the river Lethe, that would wipe away the sleeper's memory of his dream.

Special preparations were made prior to sleep to reinforce a dreamer's desire to remember a dream. The practitioner was expected to abstain from sex and from certain foods, such as broad beans, that were said to prevent dream recall. In addition, practitioners underwent ritual washing and slept on top of the skins of sacrificial animals. Once the dreamer had passed into sleep one of the sons of Hypnos would communicate a dream. Chief among these were Morpheus, who brought dreams of men, Icelus who brought dreams of animals, and Phantasus, who brought dreams of intimate things. The messages received were believed to come directly from Zeus, the father of the gods, who passed them to Hypnos and so to his sons.

The most famous place for dream incubation was the temple of Aesculapius, the god of medicine, at Epidaurus. If Aesculapius visited the temple the person sleeping therein was healed. Occasionally formulas for herbal cures would be given to the dreamer by the god. At other times he would summon sacred healing snakes to lick the wounds of the afflicted person. To encourage the god, the sleeper would put harmless yellow snakes in his bed. Aesculapius' staff branched at the top and was entwined by a single snake similar to the caduceus, the staff of Hermes with ,two serpents. To this day, this is the symbol of the physician and the emblem of the U.S. Army Medical Corps.

EXPERIMENT: Creating a Sacred Dream Space

Could it be that mankind lost the ability to recall dreams easily when a demarcation line was drawn between the logical world of waking life and the illogical world of dreams? Reason evolved and claimed the throne of consciousness and banished from memory the paradoxical world of dreams. Surely the goal of human thinking now is to integrate the intuitive powers of the past while retaining the discriminative powers of rationality. This symbiosis of reason and intuition will make us better people and more able to understand the great unanswered questions of existence. Dreams are one of the main ways to bring these psychological forces together.

We can apply many dream recall techniques of the ancients to modern life. It is unlikely that most of us would feel comfortable with sacred practices using fasting, isolation, dance and even self-inflicted pain to encourage a dream. The idea of sleeping in a sacred space may appeal, but the curators of Stonehenge, Indian sacred sites, or Greek temples probably wouldn't enjoy an influx of visitors carrying sleeping bags. And for most of us it's a long way to travel just to remember a dream!

However, having a special place reserved for receiving special dreams is achievable. If you have a spare room or attic room, it would be fun to fill it with memorabilia connected with dreams. This could include pictures of sacred dream sites, surrealist pictures and sculptures, imaginative picture-forming music, dream catchers, incense, soft lighting, and so on. If you have a particular problem you could retire to your sacred space, use some of the techniques in this book, and encourage your dream recall. This would be popular at residential New Age centers and retreats.

Having a special place reserved for dreaming would certainly show your intention to make dreaming part of your life. The same room could also be used for meditation and other spiritual practices. If a whole room is not available it may still be possible to make part of a room your special spiritual area where you could occasionally sleep on the floor in a sleeping bag.

You may have noticed that you tend to dream more when you sleep at unfamiliar places such as a friend's house, hotels, or when you go camping or on vacation. This may be partly because you have slept more lightly, but mainly it is because you have temporarily broken your habitual sleep pattern. The routines are overturned and you are more likely to interrupt a dream by waking at a time that is unusual for you. It may be as little as half an hour but it is enough to catch a dream.

EXPERIMENT:
Disrupting your routine to recall dreams

A quick and simple way to create an unfamiliar environment to encourage dreams is to sleep at the foot of the bed. Assuming that you sleep alone or that your partner doesn't mind looking at your feet all-night, it's an amusing way to encourage a dream. The disorientation you experience when you wake up and see the room from an unfamiliar perspective can act as a stimulus to make you immediately remember a dream before it fades. It may not be quite as romantic a notion as sleeping in a temple but it reinforces your decision to have a dream as you go to sleep and prompts you in to remembering one when you wake up.

This method can be very helpful when you feel the need to have a dream in order to help solve a problem that's troubling you or if you want to try one of the particular dream experiments later in this book. However, once you begin to get into the habit of routinely remembering your dreams such extreme measures may not be necessary. Nonetheless, this experiment is fun to try.

The function of dreams

The causes and meaning of dreams have been the subject of study by intelligent and learned men and women throughout the ages. Cave paintings and records from the ancient Assyrians, Babylonians, Egyptians, Greeks, Romans, and many others did a great deal to propagate dream lore. Their ideas about the meanings of dreams and their methods of interpretation and recall endured for centuries.

The general belief was that dreams were messages and visions given by the gods. Others believed that they were stories or related to the functions of the body. For example, Plato, writing in the fourth century B.C., believed that the functioning of the liver caused dreams. Similarly, Aristotle argued that dreams had sensory causes.

The Sophist philosopher Artemindorus of Dalis cataloged many of these ancient ideas about dreams in the second century AD. His set of five dream books were called the *Oneirocritica* and proved so popular, they remained in print for 1600 years. The first English translation had been reprinted 32 times by the year 1800. Some of the meanings given to dreams by Artemindorus now seem a little strange, but sometimes he comes close to modern ideas. For example, he states that many of the images found in dreams have sexual meanings. Some of his ideas sound surprisingly similar to Freud's. Similarly he recognizes that some images represent the masculine and feminine side of a person's nature, a concept that suggests the psychologist Carl Jung's theory of the anima and animus. He even proposes that some dreams are symbols. "Sometimes, there are dreams that cannot possibly happen; as when you dream that you fly, have horns, go down into Hell, and the like: These are allegorical."

Aristotle was one of the first philosophers to come close to a scientific theory to why we dream. He spoke of the soul exercising special clairvoyant powers, in accord with its divine nature, when freed from the body's constraint in sleep. However, he later claimed that the function of sleep and dreams was to dissipate the vapors that rose from the stomach after food. For many centuries it was believed that blood rose to the brain and caused congestion there. Sleep enabled the blood to drain back into the rest of the body.

Although Aristotle and others were clearly wrong about their science, they may have been correct in saying that dreams are a physiological process. Some of the latest theories propose that dreams are the body's way of "rebooting" the brain. Dreams dispose of memories that would otherwise clutter the mind with unnecessary remembered experiences. In particular they enable the emotions to become balanced.

These ideas resemble the first scientific theories from early in the 20th century, which proposed that during sleep and dreams, chemicals such as lactic acid, carbon dioxide, and cholesterol that were collected in the brain during the day were dissipated. Sleep and dreams were thought to be a function of the elimination process of the body.

Today many scientists believe that dreams are the brain's way of cleansing itself and allowing the brain's complex chemistry to stabilize. Dreams also allow the emotions to quiet down. According to this theory, without them we would simply overheat. Recent experiments with "dream withdrawal" suggest that if a person deprived of dreams begins to show psychotic tendencies while awake. In the light of this fact some scientists have proposed that the function of dreams is to allow for a time of quiet insanity. It is not sleep that is necessary for well-being, but dreams. According to this theory, we do not remember dreams because there is no need too; dreams are just psychological junk.

Sigmund Freud

Since the time of the ancient Greeks and Romans and the publication of *Oneirocritica* a great deal of research has been done into the reasons we dream. Even with this great body of scientific research nobody knows why. Today there are many psychological theories about dreams, but by far the most important pioneers of modern dream research are the Austrian psychiatrist Sigmund Freud (1856-1939) and his Swiss colleague, Carl Gustav Jung (1857-1961).

Freud believed that the purpose of dreams was to preserve sleep. He accepted the views of his predecessors that dream content consisted initially of the various sensory impressions received by the sleeper during sleep, together with the worries of the previous day and experiences of the recent past. (Aristotle in *Parva naturalia* argued that dreams were in fact fragments of recollections of events of the day.) Freud however, proposed the radical theory that to this content repressed trends or *wishes* from the unconscious attached themselves. Dreams were the attempts of these wishes to evade censorship and prevent the sleeper from waking. According to Freud the function and purpose of dreams is to gratify repressed wishes and allow us to sleep. These wishes are primarily sexual.

Freud proposed that the mind consists of three aspects, which he called the *ego, the super-ego* and the *id*. The id is the unconscious side of ourselves, which he believed consisted of instinctive drives. As the instincts always aim toward pleasure Freud called the id the *pleasure principle*. The primary pleasure principle is the urge towards sexual gratification.

Freud also identified a *"moral principle,"* which he called the *super-ego*. This roughly corresponds to the conscience. He believed this had a social origin. Living in a sexually restricted age it was natural for him to conclude that the super-ego (conscience) would be in continual conflict with the id (instinctive sexual desires). The super-ego lived in a state of constant tension, trying to control the irrational sexual demands of the id. Between these two opposites sat the conscious self, which acted as a referee between the rival claims of these two unconscious forces. Freud called this the *"reality principle"* and named it the ego. According to Freud, everyone is to some degree neurotic because the ego will never be able to satisfy the demands of both the id and the super-ego.

When a person sleeps, the ego relaxes and can no longer adjudicate between the conflicting forces of the id and *super-ego*. At this time the *super-ego* stands guard over the ego and protects it from the overwhelming instinctive urges of the id. Dreams are the symbolic language by which the id tries to communicate with the ego but its messages are censored by the super-ego. The result is that the messages from the unconscious come to the ego only in a disguised or misrepresented way.

Freud believed that the main reason people forget dreams is because they are usually too painful to remember. This is a direct result of the *censor*, the repressive ego defense-mechanism that protects the conscious mind from the overwhelming instincts and desires emerging from the unconscious.

Carl Jung

Carl Jung was the most enigmatic and controversial disciple of Sigmund Freud. He believed Freud to be wrong in many of his key assumptions about the role of sexuality within the psyche. In particular, he introduced to psychoanalysis important questions about religion and the soul that Freud neglected. Freud had become arrogant and inflexible and refused to change his views in the light of compelling evidence.

Jung realized that the unconscious was not a repository for rejected emotions and desires. He saw that the contents of dreams also showed the way to inner wholeness and healing. According to Jung, the human condition is not a continual conflict of super-ego and the id. Instead of masking hidden desires, dream symbols *express* what is going on in the unconscious. Dream symbols make an *impression* on the dreamer.

Between 1907 and 1913, Jung fell out with Freud and proposed his own theory of the unconscious. Freud had recognized that the unconscious could retain "daily residues," images from daily life that had been forgotten. But Jung noticed that some of his patients were expressing themselves with imagery from ancient traditions. He wondered if the unconscious could hold ancient or "archaic residues." Jung's patients were using inherited imagery harking back to forgotten mythologies buried in the unconscious.

In 1919 Jung called these images "*archetypes.*" He proposed a *collective unconscious* formed of instincts and the archetypes. The archetypes are inborn forms of intuition that are the necessary determinants of all psychic processes. They manifest as images. They are like primordial ideas and are numinous, electrically charged with a sense of the sacred. Many of the images are archetypal symbols originating in the collective unconscious and are powerful symbols that represent the innermost processes within the psyche.

For Jung it was entirely logical to explore the psychology of religion, astrology, alchemy, the I Ching, Chinese oracle, and other mystical traditions rejected by science. These traditions provided useful methods for investigating his patients' fantasies, dreams, and psychological problems.

Read about many of Jung's ideas in the pages that follow and realize that remembering your dreams can be a spiritually transforming process enabling you to find inner peace and psychological wholeness.

2 THE ART OF SLEEP

Oh sleep! it is a gentle thing,
Beloved from pole to pole!
To Mary Queen the praise be given!
She sent the gentle sleep from Heaven,
that slid into my soul.
Coleridge

Getting the right amount of sleep is the first step to better dream recall. If you feel rested and relaxed it will be easier to concentrate on your objective of recalling dreams. Furthermore you won't feel cheated of sleep by taking the time during the night to remember and record your dreams. (You will read about this later) By getting plenty of sleep your dream periods get longer and closer together as the night proceeds. We all dream every night, about one dream period every 90 minutes. The first dream of the night is the shortest, about 10 minutes in length. After eight hours of sleep, dream periods increase from 45 minutes to an hour. If you can establish a good sleep pattern you will gain great psychological and physiological benefit. Perfect sleep will also help you to awaken feeling refreshed and restored and will increase your energy and alertness throughout the day. In addition, it will put you in harmony with yourself, reduce the risk of nightmares, and improve your ability at dream recall.

Archaic man would rise with the dawn and sleep soon after dusk. It is only recently that this pattern has been disrupted. Today insomnia and sleep disorders are common problems. A great many people now suffer from these conditions caused by unsociable working hours, stress, worry, and the pressures of modern life. Poor sleep causes drowsiness during the day, which leads to accidents in the workplace, lack of job satisfaction, irritable moods, and arguments. In addition, it affects health and the heart, brain, and digestive system suffer.

Causes and cures of insomnia

Coffee, tea, soft drinks, alcohol, nicotine, and cold and diet medications can contribute to sleeping difficulties. Some people forget that coffee is not the only drink containing caffeine. Tea, chocolate and cola drinks are also high in caffeine. If you take prescription drugs and are experiencing insomnia, you may want to ask your doctor if they are contributing to your inability to get to sleep. Insomnia is also associated with depression, anxiety, and stress. Clearly if these conditions persist you may want to seek medical advice. However, certain herbs can help combat these conditions and with better sleep you are more able to overcome these problems.

Traditional herbal remedies include sage, chamomile, valerian, catnip, and hops. Try a cup of hot chamomile, catnip, anise, dill, passiflora, catnip, lemon balm, or fennel tea. All contain natural ingredients that will help you sleep. Most health food stores have special blends of herb tea designed to soothe you and help you get to sleep. Lavender aroma in the bedroom is also soothing and is claimed to aid sleep.

Herbal infusions to aid sleep

Hops tonic

Hops are available from home brewing shops and herbs from herbalists. Mix together equal amounts of hops, pulsatilla, cowslip flowers, and vervain. Weigh out approximately 1oz of the mixture and put in a pan. Pour on about one pint of boiling water until all the herbs are covered. Leave to stand for 20 minutes. Stir frequently. Strain the liquid. Take one small glass 3 times a day. This infusion reduces stress and aids restful sleep.

Egg Flip

This was my grandma's favorite--minus the whiskey--to help me sleep as a child. Add 1 teaspoon of sugar to a well-beaten egg. Add warm milk and stir. This drink tastes great with a small dash of whiskey or brandy. Alcohol however is not an aid to sleep. It may get you to sleep quickly but as the effect wears off your body provides extra adrenaline to compensate for the alcohol, overriding the sleep hormones. The result is insomnia.

Valerian root

Crush a valerian root, which you should be able to buy from a herbalist. Infuse in hot water and sip a maximum of one cup each night before bedtime. Evening primrose oil or crushed evening primrose root made into an infusion is also aid restful sleep. Grape juice, lemon juice, or peppermint essence in a cup of warm water are also traditional herbal sleep remedies.

Onion delight

Garlic and onion help you sleep. Slice an onion and put it into a jug. Add boiling water and leave to infuse. Strain and drink a cupful of the liquid while it is still warm.

The most common cause of a bad night's sleep is mental overstimulation before bedtime. Avoid demanding, stressful activities for a few of hours before you retire. This isn't the time to tackle emotional problems, sort out the bills, or start your tax return. Violent films on TV and even the late news can leave you feeling anxious or stressed. Instead, do something relaxing such as listening to gentle music or reading a not-too-racy book. (You can also try the relaxation techniques discussed later in this section.) If you have a cassette or CD player that will switch itself off, play soft music that will lull you to sleep. Music is available that is designed for this purpose. Similarly, sound recordings of waves rhythmically breaking or the steady pattern of a heartbeat can also do the trick.

The last things you do in the evening and the last feeling and thoughts you have before going to bed will influence your sleep pattern throughout the night. Don't spend this time struggling with conundrums or worrying about problems. An hour spent preparing for sleep or gently winding down will work wonders for the night ahead. For some people anger and resentment are like a "wide-awake pill." In particular domestic tiffs before bedtime can ruin a night's sleep. It is important to manage your anger so it doesn't harm others or ruin your own health. My Indian guru, Sathya Sai Baba, says of it: "When you are agitated by anger or hatred or agony drink cold water; lie down quietly; sing a few Bhajan songs. Or walk some long distance alone, fast, so that the pestering thoughts are driven into silence."

Noise can also interfere with your sleep. Although fresh air helps you sleep, you may want to close the bedroom windows or use earplugs if you are easily awakened by sound. A room temperature between 60-65 degrees Fahrenheit will give you the best sleeping conditions. Some people listen to white noise throughout the night. White noise is the hiss when the TV or radio isn't tuned in properly. It has been found that gentle white noise from a radio can help people with sleeping problems.

Food to help you snooze

Your pattern of eating will also affect the way you sleep. The body has natural biological rhythms that allow it to anticipate large meals by providing enzymes before the food arrives to aid digestion. However, many people are out of step with these natural rhythms and the result is heartburn and gastroesophageal reflux, which occurs when acid escapes from the stomach and travels back into the esophagus or mouth. Shift workers are particularly prone to this condition as their natural biological rhythms are perpetually disrupted.

The timing of your meals is important. If you eat too soon before going to bed your metabolic rate and body temperature will increase when they should be decreasing. This makes it harder to get to sleep. It is wise not to eat a large meal within two hours of bedtime. The best routine is to have a large meal during the day and a small meal or snack in the evening. Early afternoon is a good time for a nap; the body temperature is high enough to allow the metabolic rate to slow down and drowsiness to take over. This is also the reason why we often feel sleepy after eating a large lunch.

Experiment with your food intake to determine the optimum size meal to have in the evening. If you fall asleep easily but awaken several hours later, it may be due to low blood sugar. In this instance, try a light bedtime snack of complex carbohydrates such as oatmeal, wholegrain cereal, or a small chicken sandwich. Chicken and complex carbohydrates increase the level of serotonin in the brain. Adequate serotonin levels promote deep, restorative sleep. Also, a glass of warm milk 15 minutes before going to bed will soothe your nervous system. Milk contains calcium, which calms the nerves and helps you relax.

THE "SLEEP HORMONE"

Foods that contain a substance called tryptophan, which is converted to an amino acid called L-tryptophan, promote sleep. Tryptophan is subject to various changes by enzymes making the L-tryptophan produce a brain chemical called serotonin. Serotonin is essential for sleep and has been called the "sleep hormone." Here are some tips to encourage your body chemistry to aid sleep:

1. Eat foods high in tryptophan:

Eat these foods during the day to aid restful sleep and to encourage the release of sleep hormones.

Foods high in tryptophan include: Milk, eggs, meat, nuts, beans, fish, and cheese. Cheddar, Gruyere, and Swiss cheese are particularly rich in tryptophan.

2. Eating to get to sleep

If you have trouble getting to sleep when you first go to bed, eat a high-carbohydrate meal two to four hours before bedtime. You can also include a little food high in fat in the meal as well. This will increase the release of serotonin immediately before going to bed.

Foods high in carbohydrates include: Cereals milk, cakes, candy, sugar, ice cream, dates, figs, chocolate, cakes, fruit pie, potatoes, spaghetti, honey, and jam.

3. Eating to stay asleep

Some people get to sleep but then awaken during the night. To overcome this problem the serotonin needs to be released later in the night. Eat a snack of high carbohydrates combined with some fats immediately before going to bed. Banana is a good food to include as it digests more slowly and releases the appropriate chemicals later in the night. Similarly, a warm milky drink at bedtime works very well as milk is high in tryptophan.

Foods high in carbohydrates: see above.

Foods high in fats: cream, high-fat cheese, meat, saturated margarine, butter, peanut butter, nuts, sausages, milk chocolate, and butter.

Preparing to sleep well

Getting comfortable is also important if you want a good night's sleep. Some authorities say that it is best to sleep on your back, as this is the best position for relaxing. It allows your internal organs to rest properly. If you prefer to sleep on your side, the right side is considered best as the left causes your lungs, stomach, and liver to press against the heart. The worst position is to sleep on your stomach as this causes pressure on the internal organs. In particular, the lungs are adversely affected and you can only breathe in a shallow way. This position can also cause a stiff neck and upper back problems.

It is also been shown that exercise in the afternoon may enhance sleep, but exercise in the evening causes restless sleep. People with jobs that require a high degree of mental work and concentration are the most likely to suffer from insomnia and can benefit most from about 15 minutes of exercise during day. Aches, pains, and discomfort can also interfere with sleep. Make sure your bedroom is a comfortable temperature, and put on more blankets rather than leaving the heat on overnight. Also make sure your mattress is comfortable. One of the best ways to combat tension is simply to take a warm bath with Epsom salts before retiring.

Larks and owls

Different people need different amounts of sleep, depending on their personality and lifestyle. We don't all need the standard eight hours. Research indicates that most people require an average of eight to nine hours of sleep per night. While some people only require six hours of sleep per night, others may require as much as ten hours. Many well-known people such as Napoleon, Churchill, Mozart, and Edison all survived on five hours a night. My Indian guru, Sathya Sai Baba, is said never to sleep! Decide how much sleep you need based on your performance during the day. If you feel alert and function well with just a little sleep, you may not need as much sleep as some people.

Nonetheless it is still important to establish a sleep routine.

You cannot train yourself to get by on less sleep. To deprive your body of your genetically required sleep time may result in a sleep debt. If your body requires eight hours of sleep per night and you only sleep five hours, you build a sleep debt of three hours. Every night, as you continue to get less than your normal eight hours, the sleep debt builds. This creates a high "*Sleep Latency Quotient*," or a tendency to fall asleep. Most people repay their sleep debt on the weekend. Five days are the average time that a sleep debt can be incurred before causing daytime sleepiness or loss of concentration.

A high sleep debt can create periods of inattention or microsleeps, which are unintended sleep onsets. Many fatal errors, accidents, injuries, and deaths are attributed to sleep debt. Notable examples include the space shuttle Challenger disaster, the Exxon Valdez grounding, the Bhopal chemical plant disaster, and the Three Mile Island and Chernobyl nuclear power plant radioactive releases.

If you have an early circadian rhythm you are likely to get up early in the morning and do your best work at this time. Or you may be a night owl and function best during the evening. You should base your routines around your preferred bedtime. A newborn infant may require 16 hours of sleep per day. At age 2, sleep time has dropped to 12 hours. By age 6, the average sleep requirement is 11 hours. And at 18, people sleep an average of 8.5 hours per night Teenagers tend to have a late circadian rhythm, which means they prefer to go to bed late and get up late. Contrary to popular belief, the need for sleep doesn't decline with age. Older adults still need the same amount of sleep as they did when they were in their 30s and 40s. Sleep doesn't get worse as people age, but the patterns change.

Simple ways to help you ZZZZZZZZ.......

Try these seven simple techniques and soon you'll be in the land of nod.

Counting sheep. I'm afraid that this one doesn't work for most people because bouncing sheep are just too interesting. The objective is to slow down an overactive mind, so you need to do a more tedious visualization. Some people succeed by continually repeating a word or a meaningless phrase. For example you could choose the word "the." As you repeat it over and over again you gradually bore yourself to sleep. The, the the, the...zzzzzz. A far more pleasant method is to imagine a beautiful and peaceful place, perhaps with lakes, mountains, and green pastures. You could throw in a few sheep for good measure, but make sure they are asleep.

Remember being sleepy. Think about a time in the past when you were absolutely exhausted. You may want to recall a happy time such as on a holiday or after a festive event. Remember how good it was to sink into bed and drop into one of the best sleeps you've ever had. This is a very simple technique but is very effective.

Don't panic. Don't worry whether you drop off to sleep or not. This will only cause frustration. You can survive on three to five hours and catch up on your missing sleep on the weekend. Many people think they've not slept a wink when in reality they've slept many more hours that they believe.

Face North. In many mystic traditions it is believed sleep is improved if you sleep in the direction of the Earth's magnetic field. Some people believe that negative earth rays can cause a psychological condition called geopathic stress. Similar ideas are found in the Chinese art of Feng Shui. Repositioning the bed can help you identify a more auspicious place to sleep.

Wiggle your toes. Another mystic tip. Reflexology maintains that the feet are the place where all of the meridians in the body can be influenced. These are the channels of energy acupuncturists believe connect to all the body organs and regulate health and well being. If you wiggle your toes while lying in bed this will relax your whole body and aid restful sleep. Gentle wiggling will relax you at night, whereas vigorous wiggling will energize you in the morning.

Pranayama Breathing for better sleep

Yoga claims that certain breathing exercises bring good health and promote the deep feeling of relaxation necessary for meditation. Correct breathing also aids restful sleep. To a yogi there are two main functions of correct breathing: to bring more oxygen to the blood and brain; and to control the *prana*. (This is the vital life energy or life force that animates matter.) These exercises in turn lead to the control of the mind. Pranayama, the yogic science of breath control, consists of a series of exercises designed to achieve these goals and to keep the body in vibrant health.

When you are angry or scared, your breathing becomes shallow, rapid, and irregular. However, when you are relaxed or deep in thought your breathing becomes slow. Your state of mind reflects the way you breathe, so it follows that by controlling the breath you can learn to control your state of mind. Pranayama thus not only increases your intake of oxygen and *prana* but prepares the mind for meditation or, in this case, restful sleep. It also increases the levels of alpha waves created by the brain, which are produced when we lie in a relaxed, wakeful state just before going to sleep.

If you suffer from insomnia or general anxiety, take up yoga. In particular, study Pranayama in detail. Yoga breathing together with Hatha yoga exercises revitalize the body, steady the emotions, and create greater clarity of mind. Follow its teachings and you will find deep inner peace and will sleep like a baby.

As with any form of exercise, it is important not to use extreme methods to achieve your goal. Yoga is a gentle way to good health. It is particularly important to remember this when doing the pranayama exercises, or the results will not be beneficial. If at any time you feel discomfort or feel that you want to gasp for air in gulps, stop the exercises and breathe normally. If you experience feelings of extreme heat or cold while doing these exercises you are pushing yourself too far.

The exercises that follow are simplified versions of traditional yoga techniques. You should find them easy to do and an effective way to calm your mind.

BREATHING EXERCISE 1
- simple relaxation using the breath.

This is a remarkably simple technique but is very effective. By linking your breath to your relaxation, it is possible to achieve a relaxed body and mind quickly. You can use this method in any tense situation. Try it next time you're in the dentist's chair!

Step 1: Do this exercise sitting down or lying in bed. Relax very deeply and let go of all stress. Feel your body relax completely. As your breathing slows, feel your body become more and more at ease.

Step 2: Now take a slow deep breath in and as you do, think to yourself "I am…"

Step 3: And as you breathe out, think "…relaxed." Let the word "relaxed" feel like a great sigh, and allow your body to sink deeper into perfect relaxation. As you breathe out, let your whole body relax completely.

Step 4: Repeat the process a few times.

BREATHING EXERCISE 2
removing spiritual toxins

Another simple technique to remove stress and promote restful sleep involves the power of the imagination to influence your spiritual state. You can do this exercise sitting in a chair or lying in bed. This simple technique will leave you feeling purified within and help you get rid of negative feelings and influences. It is also a powerful self-healing technique.

Step 1: Let yourself relax very deeply and let go of all stress. Feel your body relax completely. As your breathing slows down, feel your body become more and more at ease.

Step 2: Take a slow deep breath in and as you do, see the air as being made of brilliant white light. Feel it spread from your lungs and fill your whole body. As it does this, you will feel warm and comfortable all over.

Step 3: Now, as you breathe out, see the air you exhale turning into arid black smoke. With it are released all the toxins from your body. Feel also how you let go of all tension, anger, depression, and any other negative feelings you have. Use your breath to remove all this negative energy from your being.

Step 4: Repeat the exercise as many times as you like, each time feeling the dark energy being removed and replaced by the soothing warmth of the incoming light. This exercise can be quite mentally stimulating but is effective at removing stress and thereby aiding restful sleep.

BREATHING EXERCISE 3
Alternate nostril breath (Anuloma Viloma)

This final example is a classic pranayama exercise that balances the body's energies. It is a little more complicated than the first two and should be done either sitting in the lotus position or in a chair. It is important that the spine, neck and head be in a straight line to facilitate the movement of the positive living energy called *prana*. This exercise also cleanses the energy channels that run down the spine called the *nadis*. You will be breathing through each nostril separately and thereby balancing the *prana* flow through the body, especially up and down the spine. This exercise also helps to stimulate the spiritual powers and can be used in conjunction with the various esoteric dream techniques that will be discussed later.

In this exercise you inhale through one nostril, retain the breath, and then exhale through the other nostril. The best ratio is 2:8:4, but work at first with whatever you feel most comfortable. Take it gently at whatever pace most suits you. You are not trying to break any records. The objective is to improve your ability to find inner peace by controlling your breath and also controlling your mind.

Step 1: Sit comfortably relaxed, with a straight back, neck, and spine.

Step 2: Tuck the index and middle fingers of your right hand into your palm and raise your hand to your nose. Place the thumb on your right nostril and your ring and little fingers by your left.

Step 3. Breathe in through the left nostril as you close the right with your thumb.

Step 4: Now hold the breath for a few seconds, closing both nostrils with your fingers and thumb.

Step 5: Breath out slowly through your right nostril, keeping the left closed with your ring and little fingers.

Step 6: Now breathe in through the right nostril while continuing to keep the left nostril closed.

Step 7: Again hold the breath as you close both nostrils.

Step 8: Now breathe out through the left nostril, this time keeping the right closed with your thumb.

Step: 9: You have now completed one round of Anuloma Viloma breathing. Repeat the exercise. At first you will probably be able to do five rounds. Soon you will feel comfortable doing ten. Build up slowly to 20 rounds

Breathing in a slow, relaxed way will greatly improve your ability to sleep.

SYSTEMATIC WAYS TO RELAX

Yoga breathing exercises are a positive way to help you relax. Similarly the physical yoga exercises can also aid restful sleep and restore a feeling of harmony throughout the body, mind, and spirit. One of the simplest exercises you can do at any time is simply to raise your hands above your head and stretch your whole body like a cat waking up from a long sleep. When you've finished, allow your whole body to relax.

Stretching helps release the tension within you. This alternate tensing and relaxing is necessary because only by knowing what tension feels like can you be sure you've achieved relaxation. By doing this you achieve a stage of mastery over your body's involuntary processes, because you've sent instruction to your muscles to relax. An adept of yoga can gain incredible mastery over the involuntary muscles of the heart, digestive system, nervous system, body temperature, and so on.

When you are completely relaxed you will have a feeling of expansion, lightness, and warmth. As muscular tension disappears it is replaced by a feeling of gentle euphoria that fills the whole body. Relaxation is a gradual process, and you will feel yourself sinking deeper and deeper into this blissful state of being.

Even a few minutes of deep relaxation will reduce worry and fatigue and will promote restful sleep. The exercise that follows is a powerful visualization technique to help you relax. I use it myself at my spiritual workshops to help people prepare for meditation. (To have me talk you through this process to music, download an audio file of the following exercise from my website at http://www.psychics.co.uk) This exercise is designed to help you become aware of your body and to teach it to relax very deeply. Some people benefit by stretching and relaxing before beginning the exercise. For example, first stretch your toes and feet and feel them relax. Then stretch just your legs and feel them relax. Systematically stretch your muscles from the toes to the face until your whole body has been prepared for even deeper relaxation.

RELAXATION EXPERIMENT

Lying comfortably, feel the pressures of the day falling away. Relax very deeply and feel yourself able to let go of all stress. Deeply relax, more and more, and be aware of how good you are starting to feel. You are able to leave your worries behind because this is *your* time to enjoy *your* right to deep inner peace.

Notice how your body is becoming more and more at ease. You are probably already feeling that your breath is calming down. So it is easy now to take a deep breath in, and as you breathe out, think to yourself **"relax."** Maybe you want to do this a few times.

How would it feel if you relaxed completely?

You might notice those warm, calming sensations in your toes and feet spread through your body easing all tension.

Take your attention to your toes. Wiggle them for a while then let them relax. Be aware of how heavy they feel as they gradually relax more and more. Now move your attention to your feet and notice how they have already relaxed with the toes. Feel them become warm and heavy. Feel the tension that was once there fall away. In your feet are nerves connected to your whole body. As your feet relax feel your whole body follow suit.

Next, move to your legs. Feel the comfort and peace fill them. All tension is gone. They are completely relaxed. Now become aware that your stomach and hips are relaxed. Letting go of all stress, feel yourself moving toward a soothing cloud of enfolding restfulness.

Your whole torso is now relaxed. Your breathing is restful and your whole body has slowed down. Be aware of how comfortable your hands and arms are feeling. Are you aware how much the shoulders have relaxed? Enjoy the restful feeling in the muscles of your face, especially the muscles around your eyes.

Your whole body is relaxed.

Since you are now totally relaxed, your mind is also quieting down. Notice a growing sense of inner composure and deep peace, an all-prevailing sense of serenity and tranquility. Enjoy this glorious state of physical and spiritual peace. When you feel ready, let yourself go into perfect peace, perfect rest, perfect sleep. You are ready to dream.

3 RECALL AND EXPERIMENTATION

It has never been my object to record my dreams, just the determination to realize them.
Man Ray (1890-1976)
Surrealist artist and photographer

No-nonsense people who proudly boast "I never dream" are fooling themselves. Instead, they should be saying, "I never *remember* my dreams" for we dream every single night. Psychological tests suggest that non-recallers are often more controlled and conformist than those who can easily remember their dreams. Likewise, people who avoid facing anxieties in daily life may show a reluctance to recall their dreams. The truth is, we all dream and it is easy to remember dreams. All we need is an open mind and a few simple techniques.

Recent research indicates that we dream throughout sleep from the moment we drop off right through the night and to the time we wake up. However, the most vivid dreams occur at regular cycles that can be identified by observing the eyes.

American physiologist Nathaniel Kleitman in 1951 noticed that sometimes the eyes of sleeping infants would move rapidly from side to side behind their closed eyelids. He suggested to Eugene Aserinsky, a graduate student, to study the relationship of eye movement and sleep. Kleitman and Aserinsky soon discovered that if they woke adults at this time they would invariably say that they were having a dream. In addition, EEG readings confirmed that during REM sleep there was a recognizable change in the activity of the brain. These periods of "rapid eye movement" (REM) proved to be extremely useful as they revealed when a dream was taking place. By waking the subject during REM sleep, researchers could guarantee that there would be a dream to study.

It is now known that dreams are not confined only to REM periods but continue throughout the night. Most dream research has been based on waking people during REM sleep, but its now claimed that it is possible to recall a dream at any time during the sleep cycle. Carl Jung claimed that we are dreaming all the time—even while awake—and it is only the distractions of waking life that leave us unaware of our waking dreams.

Nonetheless, the best time to recall a dream is in the intense period of dream activity found during REM sleep. You are more likely to remember having had a dream if you are awakened at this time. It has also been found that dreams taking place during REM activity have more visual content than those occurring at other stages of sleep. It has been suggested that the brain does not distinguish between the visual imagery of dreams and that of waking life. In effect, the eyes may be watching the events of the dream as if they are taking place in reality.

RECALL METHOD
INTERRUPTING EARLY SLEEP CYCLES

Sometimes it may appear that a night's sleep is just a period of unconsciousness. One moment you're dropping off to sleep and the next the alarm clock is ringing and you're getting ready for the day's activities. However, during the hours that have passed, you have experienced a number of changes of brain activity, types of sleep and dreaming. Research has revealed that there appear to be four distinct levels or stages of sleep, each one different and characterized by distinctive brain rhythms and alterations in the bodily condition.

Dr. Nathaniel Kleitman and another of his students, William C. Dement, were the first people to study these sleep patterns scientifically. They found that during the first 15 minutes the sleeper descends through four distinct stages of sleep cumulating in the deepest, at Stage Four. This period of non-REM sleep lasts about one hour. During this time the body is at its most relaxed, with the brain rhythms at their slowest. Following this is a rapid return to Stage 1. It is then that the first REM episode of the night begins. It lasts about 10 minutes.

If you are married or have a partner, if you ask to be awakened at this time it is likely that you would recall a dream. Your partner should look for a telltale change in body posture and rapid eye movements under the lids. This method is impractical in that it might be difficult to get to sleep knowing that you'll be awakened by a bleary-eyed partner. However, if you're really keen to remember a dream, you could ask to be awakened should your partner awaken spontaneously and see that your eyes show REM activity.

Another somewhat extreme technique is to drink a large glass of water before going to bed. Inevitably, you will wake up in the night. With luck you will interrupt a REM period and recall a dream. I've tried this approach myself but unfortunately always end up dreaming about toilets!

Some herbalists suggest that you drink *Dream Recall Tea* before bed. The herbs are claimed to encourage dreaming and dream recall. Again, a full bladder will probably wake you up during the night and give you a chance to write down essential points from any dreams you've had.

To make *Dream Recall Tea* add ¼ cup of dried mugwort to 2 tablespoons of dried rosemary. Add the ingredients to 2 cups of boiling water. Steep for at least 10 minutes before straining. Sweeten with honey if desired.

RECALL METHOD
INTERRUPTING LATE SLEEP CYCLES

The most vivid dreams usually occur just before awakening and these are the best ones to interrupt, so it isn't necessary to use bladder-challenging methods. Throughout the night, the process of descent and ascent through the stages of sleep are repeated between four and seven times. This gives you many opportunities to remember a dream. As the night progresses, frequency and rapidity of eye movement increases, as does the period spent dreaming. The final dream period just before awakening up can last up to about 40 minutes.

If you set your alarm to ring up to 40 minutes early you are likely to interrupt a dream. Using the techniques described in this book, you will be able to remember it in detail. I suggest setting the alarm at different times each morning for a few days. One morning you may try the adventurous 40-minute-early session, and the next morning rise just 15 minutes early. Dream recall should be enjoyable, so don't overdo it, especially during the work week. Try three mornings in a row, perhaps including the weekend, then let your sleep pattern return to normal. Excessive REM deprivation leads to daytime irritability, fatigue, memory loss, and poor concentration. However once you get into the routine of remembering your dreams the habit will stick and you'll recall a dream most mornings with no ill effect.

REM sleep is an extraordinary state of awareness: brain activity, adrenaline levels, pulse rate, and oxygen consumption are almost the same as when you are wide-awake. However, muscle tone relaxes and it is very difficult to awaken people at this time. During REM sleep the brain is extremely active, to the point that the body has to be mostly paralyzed to prevent it from thrashing around and acting out dreams. This combination of an active brain in an immobile body so mystified the early sleep researchers, they called this state "active sleep" or "paradoxical sleep." It is considered by some psychologists to be a third basic form of human existence. This corresponds to the ancient Hindu tradition that consciousness consists of three separate states: waking, dreamless sleep, and dreaming. We will consider these ideas in detail later in the book.

RECALL METHOD
STIMULATING THE BACK OF THE BRAIN

Have you ever dreamed about being unable to run, attempting in vain to scream, or being stuck in mud or quicksand? This type of dream may be caused by the physiological changes that happen to the body and brain during REM sleep and in particular the areas of the brain that keep the body immobile during sleep. Irrespective of the dream content, during REM sleep the heart rate and breathing often become erratic, the gastric acid in the stomach increases considerably, and there is an increased tendency to cardiac arrest. In addition, limb twitches, middle-ear muscle twitches, and sudden respiratory changes occur. Men tend have a penile erection. Yet despite all this physiological and psychological activity, the body remains immobile and sleep is preserved.

So what is it that stops people from thrashing around in sleep? Animal studies have identified the locus ceruleus in the pons section of the brain as the probable source of this inhibition. (The pons is in the brain stem at the bottom of the brain directly above the medulla oblongata; the locus ceruleus borders on the brain cavity known as the fourth ventricle.) Animal experiments have shown that when this part of the brain is surgically destroyed, animals periodically engage in active, apparently goal-directed behavior during REM sleep. They appear to be acting out the content of their dreams.

Mysticism also considers this area at the bottom and back of the brain to be important for dreaming. Patanjali, the author of the Yoga Sutras (4 BC) tells us that meditation upon this area of the brain will put us in touch with celestial beings. Similarly, in Tibetan mysticism it is taught that this is the part of the brain responsible for out-of-body travel as it is linked to the throat *chakra* (center of spiritual energy). And in my own work as a Spiritualist medium, I have noticed that meditating on this area of my brain before a demonstration appears to improve the accuracy my mediumship.

As far as I am aware, no scientific research has been done into these metaphysical claims, and much of the evidence remains anecdotal. However you can test these claims for yourself. Workshop 4 will show some mystical techniques that use this part of the brain for out-of body travel and communication with spiritual guides. Prior to Workshop 4, you may want to practice with this part of the brain to increase dream activity.

THROAT CHAKRA EXPERIMENT:

Objective: To stimulate the back of the brain to increase dream activity.

Step 1: Lying flat on your back, allow yourself to relax deeply as you did in Workshop 1 in the "Relaxation and preparation for sleep" experiment.

Step 2: Visualize a brilliant blue light unfolding at the top of the throat *chakra*. This is located at the top of the throat and is a center of spiritual energy called the Visuddha in India. Its element is ether and it traditionally represents communication and self-expression through thought, writing, speech, dance, and art.

Step 3: "*Chakra*" is a Sanskrit word meaning wheel. You may now see this center spinning with brilliant blue light. Feel how the light brightens as this spiritual center floods with radiant light. The light expands and unfolds like a blue lotus flower of light. Notice how the energy here increases as you see the glittering light flood this area of your body.

Step 4: As this lotus unfolds, be aware of how the blue light now floods the back of the head. Bathe the back of your head in this beautiful, soothing radiance. Enjoy the way it brings you inner peace and calmness. Bask in the light that radiates from your throat.

Step 5: Retain the light in the back of your head but see the throat center close. It fades to darkness as the lotus closes its petals. Now go to sleep as normal.

Result: You may find that by doing this technique before bedtime you will increase the vividness of your dreams. Nobody yet knows how or why these ancient techniques work but it is claimed that they do more than plant a suggestion in the subconscious, They unlock your spiritual energies and can make dreaming part of your spiritual work..

This mystical technique may help you increase the likelihood of having a dream. Just thinking about dreams before going to sleep can also help you encourage dream recall. Read this book in bed to encourage you to remember a dream in the morning or to awaken just after you've had a dream.

Another important aspect of dream recall is to eliminate the barriers that stop you from remembering. To do this, you need to approach your dream in the right way:

DEVELOPING THE RIGHT ATTITUDE

Sometimes dream memories may elude you because you are unconsciously blocking your ability to recall them. You may have hidden fears about what your dreams reveal about your personality, attitudes, urges, and desires. Part of you doesn't want to know the truth about yourself.

Freud believed that the main reason people forget dreams is because the dreams are too painful to remember. This is a direct result of what he called the *censor*, a repressive ego defense mechanism protecting the conscious mind from the overwhelming instincts and desires emerging from the unconscious. According to Freud, the primary purpose of dreams is to prevent us from waking.

Similar ideas are postulated by psychodynamic dream theory, which says that the reason for lack of dream recall is that dreams contain things we just don't want to remember. This is material the waking self just can't cope with or that would cause too much distress if remembered. This dream material is referred to as ego toxic.

This agrees with Freud's theory that dreams are mediating desires that are seeking expression and counter forces keeping those thoughts and impulses from disturbing the sleeper. The content is disguised before reaching consciousness, but some gets kept away from the waking ego altogether. Hence the memory loss.

Many clinicians believe that the theory is useful and that the process can be observed over time. For example, new patients recall fewer dreams but as patients begin to show other signs of less resistance to the material that the dream content is displaying, more of this dream content shows up. The greater the degree of repression the lower the dream content.

The question posed by Freud remains unanswered. We still do not know whether a dream's function is to preserve sleep or whether we sleep so that we can dream. Freud's views are still a subject of debate but nonetheless it is clear that most people create barriers between the conscious mind and the world of dreams. Here are a few simple tips to help you change your attitude and make dream recall easier:

1. Enjoy your dreams. If you look forward to having a dream when you go to bed, you are more likely to recall a dream when you wake up. The more you want to dream, the easier it becomes to remember them.

2. Give yourself permission to dream. Dreams may contain material that you've repressed or pushed out of your awareness. Look forward to the reconciliation of your hidden fears. Soon you will be able to leave these fears behind you and take the first steps toward discovering your true identity.

3. See your dreams as valuable. Dreams are not a load of old nonsense. They are the key to self-discovery and personal growth. Perhaps you could repeat an affirmation to help hammer this message home. Repeat "Dreams are important to me" a number of times at regular intervals. This will encourage you, on a subliminal level, to automatically recall your dreams. A physical "trigger" along with the verbal suggestion often helps, i.e. pressing your thumb against each finger as you say each word of the suggestion.

4. Feel and accept the emotional content of dreams. Some people find sexual dreams disturbing or are frightened to uncover the truth about themselves. Accept whatever occurs in a dream and use the material to gain insight into yourself. After all, what is there to be afraid of? Everything in dreams is a part you.

5. Let dreams solve your problems. The messages from your unconscious deserve to be heard. Consider dreams to be a best friend who will help you identify your faults and capitalize on your strengths. Dreams seek to reveal the truth about you. Armed with this knowledge you can learn to change your behavior and attitude in positive ways. Also, hidden within your dreams may be simple solutions to difficult problems. Once you start drawing upon this inner wisdom, you will discover the benefits of your dream memories.

6. Be creative. The Japanese filmmaker Akira Kurosawa said, "Man is a genius when he is dreaming." Many great novels, inventions, music, paintings, and scientific breakthroughs have been directly attributed to dream insights. The more you allow your dreams to be recalled, the more creative material you will have at your disposal.

7. Examine your motives. Dreams originate from the core of your being. They reveal your true motives and desires. From a spiritual standpoint, motive is everything. If the motive is correct, good karma is generated and happiness is guaranteed. A remembered dream can put you in touch with the hidden motivations and spiritual prompting that can direct your life toward true happiness.

RECALL METHOD
THE BASICS OF DREAM RECALL

If you don't know the right techniques it can be very frustrating trying to recall dreams. Not only do most people never remember most dreams, the ones they remember can easily slip away and evaporate. However, with a little guidance and effort, you will soon remember more dreams than you know what to do with. The techniques will be explained in detail later, first consider the basic steps that will empower you to remember your dreams.

These simple recall methods will be discussed in detail soon:

1 BE PREPARED: Before you go to sleep make sure you have a pen and paper within easy reach by your bed. When you awake, whether in the

night or in the morning, jot something down. Even writing "I don't remember anything this morning" will do, but a more positive statement such as "I will remember my dream at the next opportunity" is much better. The important thing is to establish a habit of dream recall and to train yourself to remember your dreams. Your intention to have a dream and make an effort to remember it in itself will help you to recall dreams.

2 CONTEMPLATE YOUR DAY: When you go to bed, relax your body and think about the day's events in reverse order. This is a technique will teach you how to reflect and can itself be very relaxing. It will also help you remember your dreams. For example, ask yourself questions such as: "How did I get ready for bed?" "What was I doing just before going to bed?" "What did I watch on TV this evening?" "What was it like coming home from work?" "What did I do at work?" The events of the day will start to unfold naturally and you may fell like you are watching a videotape recording. Finally, you will reach the point where you woke up in the morning. Can you go back just that little bit further and remember what you were dreaming?

3 PROGRAM YOUR UNCONSCIOUS: As you get close to falling asleep, repeat, "When I wake up, I will remember my dream." The unconscious and the memory are influenced by repetition. You may think you sound stupid but actually saying the words aloud reinforces this inner command. Some authorities recommend that a physical "trigger" along with the verbal suggestion often helps. Again, try pressing your thumb against each finger as you say each word of the suggestion.

4 DON'T JUMP STRAIGHT OUT OF BED: When you wake up in the morning, lie still. Relax your body and let your mind drift. With practice, you can easily hover between waking and dreaming without falling back to sleep. Remind yourself that you *want* to remember your dream. You may prefer to keep your eyes closed or look at something bland such as the sheets close you your face. Whatever you do, don't start running through lists of what you have to do during the day. If you do, your dream will evaporate immediately.

5 WRITE, WRITE... WRITE: Most dreams are forgotten within 10 minutes so start scribbling as soon as you remember the first snippet of a dream. Write down whatever you remember immediately so you're not trying to remember that material while trying to recall new material. Do it as it comes to you or you will forget what came a few seconds earlier. Don't give yourself a chance to forget. If you prefer, review the parts of your dream in your mind once or twice before recording them on paper. Work

whichever way best suits you, but act quickly.

6 TELL SOMEONE: It is surprising how many extra details surface if you talk about your dream. Someone you can trust may even be able to help you with the interpretation. In most tribal societies it was a tradition to share your dreams with other members of the tribe.

KEY RECALL METHOD:
THE SIMPLE DREAM DIARY

The simplest and easiest way to remember your dreams is to write them down. At first, you may be content to write them onto scraps of paper or a notebook. However, if you are serious about learning dream recall, I suggest you make yourself a proper dream diary. This will give you a permanent record that can be used to cross-reference dreams over many years. Furthermore, you can identify recurrent themes and have a record of any dreams that prove to be prophetic. A dream diary is not only useful but can be a very creative and enjoyable exercise.

Start by creating a basic dream diary. Later you'll learn a more comprehensive method and may also want to introduce techniques and layouts of your own. But begin with a very simple and easy-to-use dream diary:

First, buy a large sketchbook. You will need the space later on, when you introduce sections for sketches, mind-maps, future dreams, past-life logs, and so on. Some people prefer a large loose-leaf ring binder, but a properly bound book will last for years. Some specialty art and stationery shops have them. I opted for a large corporate desk diary with one day per page. I ignore the dates.

There are also a few well-designed dream diaries on the market, but they may limit you to the techniques favored by the designers. The truth is that everyone thinks differently. What works for one person may not work for you. Later, as you learn various techniques, you will choose the methods that suit you best so your dream diary will become uniquely your own. There are no hard and fast rules. You must use whatever technique helps you the most.

In the front of my dream diary, I have written a quote by Oscar Wilde: "I never travel without my diary. One should always have something sensational to read on the train." It reminds me that creating a dream diary is fun. The absurdity of the quote also encourages me not to take myself too seriously. When you start working with the unconscious, it is important to be cheerful yet honest with yourself. In this way, you will get to know yourself better and acknowledge those parts of you that until now you have ignored. So your first step may be to find a quote or make something up that expresses the way you feel about your dream. This is not essential but it sets a creative precedent.

Always keep your dream diary beside your bed. Make sure you put it where you can see it, such as on the bedside table. If it's the first thing you see when you wake up, this will help jog your memory that you have had a dream. The first moments of waking consciousness are the critical point at which a dream is remembered or lost.

Step 1: BEFORE GOING TO SLEEP: Write the next morning's date at the top of the page. Doing this the night before will help convince your unconscious to reveal a dream. As well as being an act of faith, it also frees you to get straight on with the process of scribbling down your dream immediately when you wake up. Use the relaxation techniques from the first chapter and get in the mood for a dream. Do this as you drift off to sleep, repeating : "Tonight I will have some wonderfully vivid dreams". You may also like to read about dreams before going to sleep or read dreams you recorded from previous mornings. This may be a good time to work out an in-depth interpretation of the last dream you had from the previous morning.

Step 2: WAKING UP: Remind yourself you want to remember your dream. Shutting your eyes may help. Lie still and think about your dream. Take your time coming round; you only need a few minutes and will not be late for work. Let the dream unfold. At first stay in the same position and let the dream unfold. When you have exhausted the recall in that position, move slowly to another position that feels natural. See if your can remember anything else. If so, write it down.

Step 3: WRITE A TITLE: Give your dream a title right away or leave a space for one so you can put it in later. It should express something succinctly about the content so you can easily refer to it later. A title can also help in cataloging and locating dreams. Also, the title itself may be influenced by your unconscious and may give clues to an interpretation.

Step 4: RECORD NAMES FIRST: Quickly write down anything you heard in the dream because auditory information is the first thing to be forgotten. Include any names of streets, people, countries, and so on. In particular make a note of anything anyone said.

Step 5: DON'T WORRY ABOUT SEQUENCE: Dreams can sometimes have confusing plots that jump back and forth between times and locations. The important thing is to get as much information on the page as quickly as possible. You are not trying to write a masterpiece or your novel. Write down everything that comes to mind, even the embarrassing bits.

Step 6: FORGET SPELLING AND GRAMMAR: Concentrate on the dream. It doesn't matter if you make grammar or spelling mistakes. When something is hard to describe in words, draw a quick sketch.

Step 7: WRITE IN THE PRESENT TENSE: Write the dream as if you were experiencing it as you write. This will help keep it fresh in your mind and keep your attention focused. It also allows you to experience more closely the feelings you were having when you had the dream. Here's a simple example of writing a dream in the present tense: "I am walking toward a big building. I can see that it is old and decayed. There is a smell of dampness in the air. I hear a call 'Hey, you! What are you doing here?' It is the woman from my dream of last week. I can see that she has a flower in her hand."

Step 8: INCLUDE EVERYTHING: List everything that happens, no matter how trivial. For example, the weather in your dream may represent something about the way you are feeling, colors have special symbolic significance as do shapes and numbers. Everything you think, see, feel, smell and hear in your dream is there for a reason and says something about you. Nothing is insignificant.

Step 9: DIG DEEPER: Once you think you have everything, go back over the first things you can remember about the dream. How did the dream start? You may find a whole sequence of dream events you completely forgot about. Once you remember a small part, it unlocks the door to another dream entirely. Make notes about this dream also. When you can't remember any new material, review whatever you have written. Sometimes that will trigger forgotten parts. Ask yourself questions about it. For example: "Who else was in the dream? What color was it? How many were there? How do I feel about that? How far away was it? Was there any noises or smells? What was on my left and right? What was I wearing? What time of day was it?"

Step 10: IF ALL ELSE FAILS: If you cannot remember having had a dream, write down whatever you are thinking about. Your thoughts may be mundane or banal or about something completely removed from dreams, but write them down anyway. If you are unable to recall any images, just experience your feelings. Each morning when you wake up, you feel a little bit different. Express that feeling. The first feelings you have on awakening may be caused by your dreams. Writing down your thoughts and feelings will also get you into the habit of recording your inner world first thing in the morning. A particularly good technique is to write down a short made-up fantasy about what you would have *liked* to have dreamed about. Eventually, the action of writing will be the catalyst for a dream memory. Finally, put the title as "I will remember my dream at the next opportunity." Sometimes a dream will come back to you if you just it let go. Intentionally let the dream go, telling yourself that it will return to you within a few minutes and you will soon catch it

Step 11: FINISHING: Leave enough space below the dream for a quick interpretation now and space for a more detailed one later. At the bottom of the page, make a few notes about what is going on in your life at the moment. This will help you with your interpretation and, at a later date, to see patterns.

Step 12: ADD THE DATE: This will help you later when you want to make connections between your dreams and the events in your life.

REMEMBERING SIGHTS, SOUNDS, AND SENSATIONS

As far as we know, everybody thinks in different ways. Do you think in pictures (seeing), words (hearing), or feelings (sensing)? You probably do a mixture of all three but one of these senses is likely to dominate. For example if you respond to someone by saying, "I *see* where you're coming from," or "I get the *picture*," or "Let's get things in *perspective*," you're more likely to be a person who thinks visually.

If you were to say, "I *hear* what you're *saying*," or "That *rings* a bell," or "You're *speaking* my *language*," you're most likely to be a person who thinks in sound. However, if you respond with "I can *handle* this," or "I get your *drift*," or "I *feel* the same," you're most likely to a person who thinks with their feelings.

If you listen very carefully to a person talking you will soon notice that the person mainly use one of these senses. Once you've recognized the way the person speaks you can respond in the same way. So if you want to flatter a visual thinker, use phrases such as: "You've really *brightened* up my day," or "We *look* good together," or "You make me *shine*."

In the same way, you can influence a verbal thinker by using saying things like: "We're on the same *wavelength*," or "You're really *chirpy*," or "We seem to *click*."

With the sensory person, use words about touching, such as: "You're really *warm*," or "I like your *pushiness*," or "I'm glad we made *contact*."

These are techniques used by highly trained and motivated salespeople. Many of these persuasive techniques are also used in advertising, television, and newspaper advertising slogans. It's possible to exert a powerful influence on people by using these techniques because the person believes that you think in exactly the same way as they do. They find themselves responding to you but don't quite know why.

Dreams are primarily visual in their content. However, if you tend to be verbal or sensory during you day-to-day life, sounds and sensations may be an important part of your dreams. It is therefore very important to note these things in your dream diary to help with your dream recall.

In addition to the visual content of the dream, here are other qualities you may be aware of:

SOUNDS:

What words were spoken in the dream? Always make a note of these before you write down anything else, as words and sounds are invariably the first things forgotten.

Did you hear any sounds in the background? Traffic noise, birds singing, bells ringing, the distant sound of a ship's foghorn—all these seemingly irrelevant sounds may have an important symbolic meaning. Loud sounds and explosions may represent something your unconscious is telling you about that requires your urgent attention.

Quiet or distant sounds can represent things you are only just beginning to become aware of or that have become less important to you. For example, the sound of distant thunder may show that you are aware that problems are ahead and that you should prepare.

It could also show something you've put behind you. If you think mainly in words and sounds, noting these things first may help trigger recall of the rest of the dream.

Are their any puns in the dream? If you think in words your dreams may use visual puns to represent words. For example, you dream of drinking out of a mug. Perhaps the dream is saying that you're being taken for a "mug." A similar sentiment could be expressed if you dream of a baby octopus. It could bring to mind the saying of Phineas T. Barnum (1810-1891), "There's a sucker born every minute."

Dreams twist words and phrases in innumerable ways. A pun depends on a similarity of sound but a difference in meaning. Other examples include dreaming of the sole of the foot as a symbol of the soul, or going to Hyde Park in London to representing something you have to hide or are hiding from. Freud believed that the unconscious used puns to disguise secret fears and desires.

SENSATIONS

Did you touch anything in your dream? The sensations you experience may indicate the way you feel about yourself or an issue that's bothering you. Something with a rough, unpleasant texture may reflect the way you feel. It could mean you are treating people in a rough way or feel you are being treated roughly. It could also indicate coarseness in behavior. Your dream may be using sensation to express hidden feelings. Things may be going "smoothly,"' or you may dream of finding yourself in a "sticky" situation. If you think in a sensory way, these aspects of the dream should be recorded first.

Did you smell anything in your dream? Most of us neglect the sense of smell, but it can have significance in your dream. We talk of "smelling a rat" or the "sweet smell of success" or of "a stinking argument." As part of the discipline of dream recall make a careful note of smells in dreams. Smells are symbols for feelings being revealed by the unconscious and conditions you are just becoming aware of. Smells can often remind us of childhood or events from long ago.

What feelings and emotions did your dream reveal? If you cannot remember the content of your dream, try to relive the emotions and feelings you had when you woke up. For example, if you woke up feeling angry it was probably connected in some way with your last dream. Re-experiencing this emotion will help you remember the dream scenarios that gave rise to this feeling. Feelings and emotions are not symbols but they reveal a great deal about your attitude to the issues that are the subject of the dream.

Did you feel pain in your dream? Sensory thinkers may use physical pain to express emotional pain. However, dreams can also reveal ailments and illnesses. Often they exaggerate the condition in order to make us aware of it. The first doctors of ancient Greece believed that dreams could reveal the causes and cures of illness. Perhaps your dream is urging you to see your doctor? Make a note of the actual or imaginary pain you experienced on waking and keep a careful check on your health. Future dreams may talk about the same issues in a symbolic way.

CONCLUSION:

It is useful to include everything you experience in your dream diary. Some people make subheading at the bottom of the page saying WORDS: PUNS: SOUNDS: SENSATIONS: FEELINGS & EMOTIONS:

SMELLS: These simple reminders that encourage you to recall sounds and sensations encourage better dream recall and may be more akin to your personality type and the way you think. Of course you will need to prepare a few pages of your dream diary layout in advance in order not to interrupt the smooth flow of your writing in the morning.

How do you experience your inner world?

Most people use a combination of visual, auditory, and sensory thinking during their everyday life. The list below will help you identify your own predominant characteristics. Also observe people you know. Become aware of their language, eyes, and body posture to reveal their hidden self.

The visual thinker—You speak quickly, miss details, and often speak in a higher-pitched voice. You will use words that refer to seeing, imagination, and color. You tend to look upward when thinking, keep an erect posture, and can have jerky movements.

The verbal thinker—Your smooth language flows like music. You use words that refer to hearing, speaking and listening. Your eyes move from side to side when you are thinking. You keep your head square, have flowing gestures, and keep an upright posture.

The touch thinker—You speak quietly and slowly with long pauses. You use words that refer to touching, such as feel, touch, hold, heavy. You look down when you are thinking, like to make physical contact, and slouch slightly.

ROUTINES FOR RECALL:
Encourage yourself to dream

The act of putting a dream diary beside your bed in itself may encourage you to remember a dream. Writing something in it before you go to sleep then writing again as soon as you wake up reinforces the fact that the diary will help you to remember. Other bedtime rituals can also make stronger this affirmation to remember. For example, many people hang a Native American dream catcher by their bedside. This is a hoop that has a crisscross of patterned lines running over it with hanging beads. It is said to capture the spirit of the dreams that leave the sleeper's body. By hanging one near the bed, dreams are captured and remembered.

This may sound like hocus-pocus, but dream catchers work. They help program the subconscious before going to sleep to remember a dream and jog the memory immediately upon awakening.

Simple rituals before bedtime can help with dream recall. In "Message from Forever" author Marlo Morgan talks of a traditional Aboriginal dream recall technique:

"Mapiyal used the same procedure as the others. Taking a seashell container of water, she swallowed half and made her request for information about the object in the sky. The other half of the fluid would be consumed upon awakening to connect her conscious mind to the memory of the dream. She could then have better recall for finding meaning and direction."

You could try a simplified version of this by drinking half a glass of water before you sleep and the other half immediately upon awakening.

In Europe an old superstition says you can influence your dream by writing a note to the fairies of sleep and putting it under your pillow. In the morning look at the slip of paper and you will remember a dream. In addition it will give you the answer to the question you asked. Again this technique helps you to connect your conscious mind to the memory of the dream.

Sometimes the simplest triggers will help you remember your dreams. Have you ever been talking to someone then suddenly been reminded of a dream? It could be a simple word or the mention of a person or place that sets off the recall. Once you have one image, a whole series of remembered dream events comes flooding back to you. Once you get the link the rest follows. The key is remembering this first snippet of information. Keep your dream in the back of your mind during the day. Does something remind you of your dream? Ponder any images that you remember. Doing this will help you remain connected to your dream. If during the day, you find yourself thinking of your dream, try to remember other parts of the dream starting at that point. Also, try a little synchronicity. During the day you may encounter some element of your dream. These chance encounters can often act as triggers to help you recall other parts of your dream.

Daytime routines

It is unlikely that you will be able to dedicate the first part of every morning to writing in your dream diary. Sometimes you may forget, and there are likely to be many times when you simply oversleep and it's a choice between your dream diary and being late for work. It's easy to lose the habitual routine of dream recall. That's why it's important to find ways of remembering dreams later in the day.

One of the most effective methods is to carry a notebook with you. When a dream comes to mind, stop what you're doing and write down whatever you can remember immediately. It's important that you don't put it off, as your memory of the dream will fade just as easily as when you first awaken. The information you write in your notebook can be added to your dream diary when you get home. Collecting dreams can be fun and very satisfying. I get a slight feeling of triumph when I remember a dream. Think of the feeling of frustration when you can't remember someone's name—when the name is on the tip of your tongue but you just can't bring it to mind—and finally it comes to you. It seems to have been so obvious. And it's such a relief to remember it at last.

The simplest triggers can help you remember a dream. Put a few prompts in your environment to help stimulate your ability to remember. You could perhaps write notes to yourself to help you remember. Put them in places where you are likely to be doing jobs that don't require a great deal of concentration and where you are likely to be in a contemplative state of mind. Above the kitchen sink is a good place to start, on the mirror in the bathroom or near the bath, or on the dashboard of the car. My favorite place in on my key ring. It catches my attention when I least expect to be thinking about dreams.

The note need say nothing more that "What did you dream?" You can chose from the list of suggestions in the section "Dream Notices." If visitors ask why these notes are all over the house and all but tattooed across your forehead tell them about your methods of dream recall. One of the best ways to remember your dreams is to tell people about them. Do this as often as you can. Most people won't find you a bore so long as you also let them describe their dreams as well. It is much more interesting to talk about what you dreamed than what you watched on TV. In some cases it is much more exciting material. Most people enjoy talking about dreams. The more you talk about them, the easier they are to recall. Perhaps you and a friend could agree to call each other in the morning or meet every lunchtime to talk about and interpret each other's dreams. It could turn into a very therapeutic friendship!

DREAM NOTICES

When you place notes to yourself around the house use positive commands that encourage your subconscious to recall a dream. You should also make up your own statements as well. Write the following statements on bright yellow stickers and post them in strategic places around the house, office, and car.

"I want to remember my dream because..."
"Remember your dream NOW!"
"Did you dream last night?"
"Let events remind you of your dream."
"Realize your dream."
"I can remember my dreams."

"Did you dream this?"
"Remembering my dreams is easy."
"Nothing is ever forgotten. Every minute of your dream is there to recall now."
"I want to remember my dreams."
"It is enjoyable to remember dreams."

EXPERIMENT: STREAMS OF CONSCIOUSNESS

You will notice that often you unexpectedly remember your dreams during the day. They come to you when you are off guard. This may be because the rational mind likes to keep control during waking life and so the unconscious content has trouble getting your attention. You can get around this problem by occasionally allowing yourself to enter a fluid state of mind in which you relax and let the rational mind take the back seat for a while. Not only is the next experiment an excellent way to remember dreams, it is also a first-rate way to recharge yourself and release stress.

The objective of this experiment is to deliberately induce a state of consciousness that psychologists call hypnagogic/hypnopompic dreaming. These dreamlike states are experienced as a person falls asleep and on awakening, respectively. In this state there can be an incredible flow of visual imagery before the mind's eye. It could be called a visionary experience. Sometimes the pictures and images are so vivid, the dreamer believes he is actually wide-awake and having hallucinations. They may be visual (such as seeing scenes or figures) or auditory (such as hearing your name called). A frequently occurring hypnagogic hallucination is the sensation of loss of balance, often accompanied by a "dream" of falling. This is sometimes followed immediately by a jerking reflex recovery movement (the myoclonic jerk) that may jolt the sleeper back into full wakefulness.

Using imagery to help you remember

Treasure whatever you recall. It is part of you that was once lost. Also understand that your dream images are perfect! With practice, you will develop your ability to recognize their perfection. You could construct an image of yourself recalling your dreams or use an imaginary scenario to help with your recall. For example, if trying to remember dream scenes feels like fishing, then see yourself fishing when you are recalling dreams. Other images may feel more suitable. Every time you remember, see it as scoring at golf or your favorite sport. You could imagine yourself opening a container to see if anything is inside. Or you could be on a TV game show answering questions about your dreams. Perhaps it's like watching a movie that's slowly playing backward. The best image will be the one you make up for yourself.

In the next experiment you are going to use the hypnagogic state of mind to help you connect with your dreams. You will enter a light hypnagogic state of mind while remaining fully alert and in control. You will not experience hallucinations or waking dreams but should witness a wonderful flow of incredible imagery in the mind's eye.

These amazing visions are sometimes experienced in the deeper levels of meditation. For example the mystical writer P.D. Ouspensky, who was a pupil of the guru Gurdjieff, believed that his initial spiritual preparation to receive instruction came as a child when he would spontaneously experience this high state of consciousness. He discovered that it was possible to remain in a semi-waking state in which dreams continued and could be observed. The philosophy that he and Gurdjieff later taught was that human beings are basically asleep even when we believe ourselves to be awake.

The following experiment can be spiritually significant and a helpful way to connect with your dreams. It is also a step toward lucid dreaming, which you will read about in later chapters.

Step 1: As with many other experiments, first relax completely. Set aside a special time to work with your dreams and choose somewhere where you will not be disturbed or distracted by noise. As part of your ritual you may want to light a candle and some incense to set a contemplative mood. Also, choose a comfortable chair or sit on the floor propped up by cushions. Get yourself as comfortable as possible.

Step 2: Now let the feeling of relaxation spread through your whole body. Feel a warm sensation in your toes and feet spreading upward, relieving all stress. Notice how your shoulders become relaxed and how all the pressures of the day fall away. Let the tension fall away, especially around the eyes.

Step 3: Once you are completely relaxed you will notice how your mind slows down and becomes at ease. Let go of all worries and notice your imagination beginning to activate. You may see pictures and images arising in your mind's eye. Allow the moving images to come and go. They may move from the left or right of your peripheral vision. Don't try to hold or follow the images. Let them rise and fall. When thoughts come to mind observe them, then let them go. If emotions well up observe them and then let them go.

Step 4: Now draw the images toward you and let them become exceptionally vivid. You may fix on one and look at it in detail. Look at it from above or become aware of its shape, texture, and color. Let the image become super-real, then let it drop away as you move on to the next spontaneous vision. Let your consciousness flow. Try not to fall asleep but remain in this state between waking and sleeping. You may see frightening or unpleasant images, but treat them with the same detached attitude as you did the beautiful visions. Let thought rise and fall like a gentle sea. The more you relax, the more vivid the images become. It's like dreaming, but you are wide awake.

Step 5: At first the images will be a complete muddle of strange landscapes, faces, and pictures. They may seem to have very little bearing upon you or your life. This type of conscious dreaming does not have the complicated story lines of the dreams you normally experience during sleep. However, this level of awareness gives you an insight into the creative mental processes that stir in the depths of the unconscious. Practicing this technique will help you get in tune with these inner forces.

Step 6: You will probably feel extremely relaxed when you finally switch into this state of mind. Sometimes playing gentle music such as New Age, ambient, quiet classical, or Baroque can help you hold this state. In particular ambient music is subtle enough to give you a means of holding the attention but not intrusive enough to break the flow of your consciousness. The temptation will be to fall asleep, but try to resist and stay awake.

Step 7: Stay in this state for as long as you wish. Afterward think about the images that came to you. They will fade very quickly, probably too quickly to be able to write much down. However this experience will help you spontaneously recall dreams you have already had just recently. It is likely that many fragments will have been given you as you did the experiment. Sometimes you will emerge from a session feeling relaxed and clear-headed but on other occasions you will have a head full of dream memories that can be written down and worked with. Some of these will be snippets from recent dreams, some will be from long ago, and some will be completely new ones.

The state of mind you have experienced is hard to describe and for many people hard to trigger. However, with practice you will be able to enter it at will. The knack is to let go of the thoughts yet remain fully conscious. It is tempting to follow them or be drawn in by their strange beauty. Deep relaxation, the type where the body feels heavy and distant, can also aid this state of mind.

Some authorities believe that visionary hypnagogic states are a product of the ego's attempt to regain control over thought process after the rapid change in consciousness caused by the loss of contact with waking reality. My own observation of this state is close to what can be experienced in deep meditation. It is like the blissful state that can occur when you finally let go of the thoughts and just observe them rather than being drawn along by them. Similarly in this state you are free of worry and overexcited emotions. Instead of thoughts and feelings controlling you, you can now control them. It is clearly a step toward self-mastery.

An additional benefit is that this state of consciousness can also be tremendously relaxing and within 10 minutes can completely refresh you. This state of mind can draw you away from the pressures and stress of waking life and promote personal growth and development. This dreamlike state does not have the narrative and emotional complexity of ordinary dreams and can give you the opportunity to observe your unconscious as if you were seeing it on a TV screen. It can open up your spiritual insight and creative talent. Later you will learn how to use a similar technique to gain insight into the future.

THE INK BLOT TECHNIQUE

Sometimes when a person awakens from a hypnagogic or hypnopompic dream the imagery in the person's mind is projected onto the environment. The bedroom walls can turn into a cinema screen with incredible pictures unfolding like a film. You may have awakened from a dream and seen a sinister figure or face in the folds of the curtain or in a pile of crumpled clothes. The mind will often project pictures into random shapes. For example, as a child you may have allowed your imagination to create fantastic scenes, strange faces, and weird mythical beings in the puffy white shapes of cumulus clouds against a blue sky.

These changing images come from the unconscious and are projected by the mind onto the random shapes. The pictures formed reveal the hidden processes from deep within you and the thoughts being generated by your innermost self. The pictures are keys to your dreams.

If you gaze at any random pattern, you are soon likely to start seeing faces and pictures in its haphazard form. Many people claim they can see a face in the shadows of Mars or in the patterns on the moon's surface. Similarly, you may notice that when you look at the coals of a fire, the patterns in sand, a rock formation, the gnarled bark of a tree, pictures are revealed in their shapes. Psychics use random shapes such as tea leaves, hot coals, smoke patterns, or the flaws in a crystal ball to project the images from their intuition.

While working with adolescents in a Swiss psychiatric hospital,

Hermann Rorschach noticed that certain children gave characteristically different answers to a popular game known as Blotto (Klecksographie). The game involved looking at inkblots to see who could see the most interesting pictures in the random shapes. It struck Rorschach that what the children were seeing revealed a great deal about their psychological condition. From this simple game, he devised the Rorschach Test, which today is considered one of the best psychodiagnostic procedures and an indispensable tool of psychiatry. In 1921, Rorschach published his ideas in his book *Psychodiagnostik*.

The modern Rorschach inkblot tests involve complicated procedures to study the personality and the unconscious. They use specific cards with specific interpretations to each area and clearly define interpretations to the possible responses to the printed inkblot shapes. However, inkblots can be used outside the psychiatrist's room as a means of accessing the unconscious and are an excellent way to help you remember your dreams.

In this next experiment you will use the shapes you see in a random inkblot to trigger dream recall.

INKBLOT EXPERIMENT
Making your ink blot

Step 1: It is simple to make a suitable inkblot. You will need India ink, watercolor paper, a paintbrush, and water.

Step 2: Flick ink from your brush onto the paper. Now flick about the same amount of water onto the page. You will probably need to try this a few times until you get the right proportions of ink to water.

Step 3: Fold the paper in half and press it together on a flat surface. Using a thick book, press it flat. Now unfold the sheet and allow the symmetrical inkblot to dry.

The inkblot may look a little like a butterfly or an insect. Try also just flicking ink close to the edges of the page but leaving the center blank. In this way you get other strange shapes that will suggest less obvious images. The objective is to get plenty of gray tones and contrasting areas of black and white shapes.

EXPERIMENT
Using the inkblot to recall dreams

Step 1: Put the inkblot inside your dream diary beside your bed. Use one of the techniques in this book to help you remember a dream. For example, as you get ready to go to sleep, say to yourself "Tonight I will remember my dreams."

Step 2: If you wake up and remember a dream, log it in your dream diary in the normal way. If you cannot remember a dream, then lie in the same position for a while and allow yourself to drift between sleeping and wakefulness. Continue to relax and allow your mind to float. This will give your intuition a chance to draw a dream to your attention. Allow yourself time for a dream to form in your mind. Do not start planning your day.

Step 3: Continue to keep your attention on remembering your dreams, and remain in a state as close to sleep as possible. Now look at the inkblot and allow the pictures to form. You'll notice that the pictures appear in the inkblot more easily when you are in a sleepy state. Don't try too hard. Let your mind drift and allow the pictures to form spontaneously. Look at the shapes made by the ink but also observe the negative shapes made by the white paper. Turn the page upside-down or sideways and see what other shapes are formed. Look also at the images you see in the smallest details of the inkblot. It may help to gaze at the page and watch what appears as your eyes go out of focus.

Step 4: As the pictures form you will be reminded of similar pictures that were in your dream. The inkblot will act as a sounding board and the images revealed will be very close to those found in your last dream. The more you allow your imagination to work with the shapes, the more of the dream you will remember.

You can also use an inkblot to help you recall a dream during your normal waking day. In fact any random shape can be used to encourage recall. For example, the pictures you see in a coal fire, clouds, random patters of tea leaves or coffee grounds can all form pictures. The images you see are projected from your unconscious mind. They tell you something about yourself. Just as dreams do.

Talking to invisible dream friends

The inkblot method works well because it enables you to give expression to your dream in a concrete way. It externalizes your dream. This process can bring previously unconscious material to the conscious mind and can help dream recall.

Children who have suffered physical and sexual abuse are usually encouraged to talk to dolls and teddy bears about their ordeal. This method provides a way of expressing what happened without fear of interrogation or adult reprisal. Children will tell their dolls things that would be very hard to confess to an adult therapist. A similar technique can be applied to dream recall.

Again, by externalizing the dream you can bring unconscious memories to the surface.

"AS IF" EXPERIMENT:
Externalizing your dream

Step 1: Sit in a comfortable armchair with another chair within view of you. Imagine that sitting in the chair opposite is someone who is a personification of your dream.

Step 2: The person you imagine could be someone who you remember dreaming about or someone who represents the dream in general. Act as if a real person were in front of you. If you can recall any snippets of your dream include these in the personification. For example, I recently had a vague recollection that my dream was set in Israel, but I couldn't remember anything else. I therefore chose my fantasy character to be Woody Allen dressed as rabbi whom I then cross-examined about the dream. (Choosing a fun character makes this technique more vivid and helps you not be too serious about yourself.)

Step 3: Ask the imaginary person about your dream. To continue the example of the Woody Allen rabbi, I then asked him: "Why can't I remember my dream?" He replied: "My boy, you got up too quickly. Already you missed an important dream about the Holy Land. The dream is about your spiritual path." My fantasy wouldn't win an Oscar but it worked, and important dream information was given to me very quickly. You just ask the question then let your imaginary figure give an answer. You can speak out loud if you prefer although I've found that it's quite adequate to do this whole exercise with the imagination.

Step 4: Ask a variety of questions. You may for example ask about how the dream influences your feelings and ask about the details of the dream. My own dream about Israel reminded me of the happy days I spent working on a kibbutz and the freedom I felt. Spirituality should be like this—free and happy. My dream figure pointed out to me that I was becoming too serious and ponderous about my spiritual work. Everywhere should be a Holy Land.

Step 5: Ask the fantasy character to bring forward other people from the dream. In my own case, the rabbi example showed me other characters from my dream I could then cross-examine as well. Now I could play "as if" with a whole cast of characters.

Step 6: Ask your dream characters to interpret your dream for you. You could ask them what they represent about your own personality or circumstances. Ask them why they appear in your dream and what they are trying to tell you about yourself. You could ask: "Who are you and what is your reason for being in this dream?" Once you get into the swing of this internal dialogue you will find that it a very effective way not only to recall your dreams but to understand them as well.

Step 7: If you find it hard to imagine a fantasy figure, try out the technique by talking to a doll, to yourself in the mirror, or to a photograph of someone you admire. For example, I find it helpful to talk to a photograph of my spiritual guru, Sathya Sai Baba. Sometimes answers are given to me via my inner voice that contain the solutions to problems that have dogged me for years.

QUESTIONS TO ASK YOUR INVISIBLE FRIEND

"Who are you and why are you in my dream?"
"What part of me do you represent?"
"Who else is in my dream? Can you introduce me to them?"
"What does the dream mean?"
"What should I be learning from this dream?"

Drawing Dream Doodles, Mandalas, and Mind Maps

Drawing and painting are excellent ways to get in touch with your inner self and are often used in therapy to help subjects express themselves. Many famous men and women have used art as therapy. Sir Winston Churchill was an accomplished painter, for example, as was Adolph Hitler. Recent famous amateur painters include Prince Charles, John Lennon, David Bowie, Jade Jagger, Jayne Seymour, and Sylvester Stallone.

Art can be a direct route to the unconscious, particularly if you allow yourself to be influenced by whatever your imagination sends you. Art that is spontaneous rather than meticulously planned is often influenced by the unconscious. Sometimes unconscious symbolism creeps into a work without your conscious realization it has happened. For example, art critics observe that the paintings of Van Gogh express his psychological state of mind. The dark crows that cower above a swirling sea of wheat, a spiraling night sky, or a solitary white iris all express his inner turmoil and loneliness. However, Van Gogh may have been completely unaware of the subtle symbolism that he was including in his paintings. These moving symbols may have arisen spontaneously as Van Gogh immersed himself in the creative process.

Mysterious unconscious imagery appears in the work of many of the world's great painters. The works of Hieronymous Bosch, Titian, El Greco, William Blake, Henri Rousseau, Holman Hunt, Paul Klee, de Kooning, and thousands of others all have subtle symbolism I'm sure did not arise by conscious choice. (The main exceptions are the surrealist artists such as Salvador Dali, Max Ernst, and others who were consciously influenced by the works of Freud and other psychologists.) Art is like dreaming. It brings to light the unconscious workings of the soul.

You may not be able to draw or paint like the Old Masters, but everyone can doodle and sketch simple drawings. These drawings, which come when you are not thinking about what you are doing, can be a doorway to the hidden you. Doodling enables you to access your unconscious and is an excellent method to help you recall your dreams.

Simple doodles and scribbles reveal the way you feel. When you are thinking about something else, on the telephone for instance, you may tend to doodle. The doodle reveals your unguarded personality traits. The subconscious flows onto the paper and only needs to be read. By interpreting your doodles you can learn a great deal about yourself and the home truths that they conceal.

SOME COMMON DOODLES AND THEIR MEANINGS

- CROSSES: This may reveal that you feel angry about an issue or person. You want to remove something from your life.
- CHECK MARKS: This shows your approval. It may also show your desire to do things in an orderly way.
- SPIRALS: A spiral moves inward and shows your introspective side.
- CONTINUOUS LOOPS: You may feel that your life is repetitive and monotonous.
- CIRCLES: This illustrates your agreement. You are in harmony. It can illustrate your desire to conclude a matter. It may also show that you feel that you are running around in circles!
- SQUARES: This could show that you are searching for stability.
- TRIANGLES OR ARROWS: Upward pointing may reveal your ambitions, downward may show your disappointments. Similarly, arrows may show similar qualities.
- ANIMALS: The animals you draw may express your feelings. For example, a bird may show your desire to escape (perhaps from a

boring meeting); a bull may express anger; a snake or snakelike squiggle may reveal sexual feelings or mistrust; a cat may symbolize intuition; and a fox, cunning.

- PEOPLE: Matchstick drawings of people may show that you are thinking about or concerned about social issues. If the people are fighting you may be itching for a battle with someone. If you mutilate them this may show that you harbor a hidden resentment toward someone. The scenario that surrounds your matchstick figure reflects the way you feel about your own life and the people you know.
- BUILDINGS: People often draw simple houses similar to those we drew as children. Buildings can represent the self and also the human body. A large house may show self confidence, even egotism. A small house may show that you feel insecure or just want to go home!

The above section gives you a few interpretations for some of the more common doodles people scribble. Interpret your doodles as messages from your unconscious. What do the shapes and images represent about the way you are feeling? Perhaps they remind you of something you were dreaming about. Just like dreams, these simple pictures are messages to the conscious self from the unconscious mind. Sometimes the pictures you create can be a direct reference to a dream you recently had.

It's best to doodle when you're distracted and not consciously thinking about what you're doing. Try it while you're on the telephone or at a dull corporate meeting. Scribble while watching TV or waiting on line. Don't think too much about what you're doing. Some people find that doodling brings interesting results if they use the other hand and not the one they normally use. If you're right-handed, try doodling with your left hand. The nerves that use the left hand are connected to the side of the brain that is holistic and intuitive. Consequently the images you draw are spontaneous and come direct from the unconscious side of yourself.

Mandalas

Psychologist Carl Jung encouraged his patients to draw. He discovered that as their therapy progressed the images would also evolve like a visual story. Often this method would trigger a series of dreams changing and evolving parallel to the progress of the art. Jung found that art therapy helped his patients understand their dreams and encouraged new dreams to emerge.

Carl Jung was intrigued by the fact that many of his patients, without any prompting, drew mandalas. "Mandala" is a Sanskrit word for "magic circle." Mandalas are used in Eastern art as a means of meditation and are characterized by a circle and a square that radiate from a central point. Some of the examples found in countries such as Tibet are magnificent works of art that are considered very sacred.

Mandalas appear spontaneously all over the world. For example the great rose window in Notre Dame Cathedral in Paris is a perfect sacred mandala. Carl Jung interpreted mandalas as an archetypal expression of the self and wholeness. Mandala images often emerge spontaneously in dreams. With a mandala everything returns to a single central point. Jung believed that this symbolized that the goal of psychological development is the "path to the center." The circular structure of the mandala represents the self, which is the totality of the individual. It includes both the conscious and unconscious sides of the psyche and gives the individual a sense of meaning and purpose as the seeker moves toward it.

Jung spent a great deal of time sketching mandalas of his own. In his autobiography *Memories, Dreams, Reflections*, he says: "My mandalas were cryptograms concerning the state of the self which were presented to me each day. In them I saw myself—that is, my whole being—actively at work....The self, I thought, was like the monad which I am, and which is my world. The mandala represents this monad, and corresponds to the microcosmic nature of the psyche."

In 1927 Jung had a dream that confirmed the symbolic importance of the mandala. He dreamed he was in Liverpool. The various quarters of the city were arranged around a square. In the center was a round pool, and in the middle of it, a small island. The air was murky but the central island blazed with sunlight. In the very center stood a beautiful magnolia tree.

The name Liverpool Jung understood to mean "the pool of life" (the "liver" according to an old view, is the seat of life, that which "makes to live.") Jung continues: "The dream brought with it a sense of finality. I saw that here the goal had been revealed. One could not go beyond the center. The center is the goal, and everything is directed to the center." (Jung wrote at length about mandalas in *Psychology and Alchemy* and *The Archetypes of the Collective Unconscious* and also in his foreword to a Chinese alchemy book called *The Secret of the Golden Flower*.)

Mandalas are a good way to get in touch with the unconscious because they are symbols. By sketching them during your free time they will help reveal the images that are trying to emerge from the unconscious, the same images that are occurring in your dreams.

EXPERIMENT Drawing a mandala.

Mandalas can occur as spontaneous psychic events at times when you are attempting to integrate discordant elements within your personality and when disintegration is threatened. They help you find harmony within yourself. Using their structure as a framework for doodling and sketches encourages you to recognize the images that occur as being part of you.

Step 1. You can simply sketch your ideas with pen or pencil directly into your dream journal. If you get really inspired you may want to buy paint, paper, or canvas and turn your inspiration into something special. Many of the mandalas produced by Jung's patients are very beautiful. You may also enjoy looking at pictures of sand paintings by Native Americans or the incredibly intricate designs of the Tibetans. Your mandalas can be simple doodles or works of art.

Step 2: Think about your layout. Traditional designs are usually based around a circle divided into four or multiples of four. Tibetan mandalas often contain three concentric circles painted as a rim in black or dark blue. They are meant to shut out the outside and hold the inside together. Often these enclose a square-walled courtyard with four gates. In Tibetan mysticism this signifies sacred seclusion and concentration. These enclose the colors red, green, white, and yellow, which represent the four directions. The center is usually marked off by another magic circle symbolizing the objective or goal of contemplation.

Step 3: Your mandala can be whatever shape you like. All you need to do is lightly map out a simple framework and your unconscious will give you ideas to fill in the rest. You could start with a squared circle divided into four quarters across the center of the circle.

Step 4: Once you've planned your basic layout, fill the spaces with any shapes or images that come to you. These can be abstract, such as lotus flowers, squares circles, repeating patterns, and so on. You may include pictures of animals, faces, figures, or any images that pop into your head. At this stage, don't worry whether the images relate to dreams you've had, just enjoy jotting down whatever pictures come to mind.

Step 5: When you've finished, sit comfortably and prop your drawing in front of you. Consider each of the shapes or images and let your mind make associations with each one. For example, you may have drawn a tree within the shape of the mandala. It is there for a reason. Your unconscious has given you this idea because it is connected with an inner message. Think about what things you associate with the tree. What sort of tree is it? Does it bear fruit? Is it old or young? Does it remind you of any events in your life? Does it represent something about the way you feel? In this example a tree may symbolize spiritual growth, strength, or stability. Perhaps you associate mythical stories with the image you have drawn. You can interpret the images in your drawing in the same way you would a symbol from a dream.

Step 6: Ask yourself whether anything in the picture reminds you of a dream you've had recently or in the past. Any parts that remind you of a part of your dream can be contemplated to help you recover these lost memories. If you are reminded of a past dream, consider whether it also reminds you of more recent dreams. Are you experiencing today similar emotional conditions you did when you had the past dream?

Step 7: Finally, note your observations in your dream journal. Give your entry a title and date, and log the information in the same way you would a normal dream. You may want to make a note to say that this is a "recovered dream using a mandala."

Dream Maps

The architecture of the brain is incredible. It is estimated that we each have about one million, million (1,000,000,000,000) brain cells (neurons). Every one of these is connected to others by thousands of threadlike tentacles called dendrites and axons. It has been calculated that the number of possible combinations/permutations in the brain, if written out, would be 1 followed by 10.5 million kilometers of zeroes.

It appears that the brain works by connecting everything together like the mycelium of a mushroom. Thought cuts through this jungle of connections, and a biochemical electromagnetic pathway is formed. Every time you have a similar thought the pathway is reinforced as the connections between the cells becomes greater. This theory explains why repetition is the best way to remember things or establish a behavior pattern. Whether you learn your multiplication tables by rote, practice a sport, or repeat a spiritual mantra you are establishing patterns of thought. Repetition of mental events increases the probability of further repetition.

Dreams, like conscious thoughts, leave traces in the brain. It may be that they fade quickly because of their surreal unusualness. For example, I once dreamed of traveling by bicycle to the star Sirius. This clearly has never happened to me so it is not a memory that has been established by habit. Bizarre dreams may not leave deep memory pathways through the forest of the dendrites and axons. They are not going to be easy to access because the pathways made by unfamiliar experiences leave faint traces that are hard to find.

However, if you can remember one small fragment of your dream it can provide you with a link that connects you to the other parts of the dream. To continue the analogy of the path: it's like finding one part of a trail then systematically looking for clues to retrace your steps. This next method works well because it functions in a similar way to the brain itself. Just as the brain cells are connected together so too are the memories of a dream. Once you find a marker you can follow it back from one dream event to another.

So get out your old Davie Crockett hats to sniff out the hidden pathways of dreamland.

EXPERIMENT: CREATING DREAM MAPS

Step 1: You need a snippet of a remembered dream to work with in this experiment. For example, you may only remember that your dream was set in Switzerland and that you were eating something. Write this snippet in the center of a blank page of your dream diary. "Dream of being in Switzerland eating something" Now draw an oval around it.

Step 2: Now draw two separate branch lines to two new ovals. Put one above your original oval and one below. Write "Switzerland" in one and "eating" in the other. If you remember more than a couple of snippets of the dream you can add more ovals connected by lines to the central oval. Break what you remember into as many components as possible.

Step 3: Now draw new branch lines and ovals from each oval with associated words in them. Ideally, from these associations you will recognize something from your dream. To get started, write down anything that comes to you. For example, from the oval "eating something" you may link things like cheese, chocolate, fondue, or any of the foods you may associate with Switzerland. You can continue by writing down other foods that spring to mind—pizza, chewing gum, pastrami, and so on. You can also ask yourself where you were eating and what time of day it was. Note also your feelings associated with the dream snippet. Put each into an oval from the "eating" oval. You can of course go on forever, so limit yourself to about 12 associations.

Step 4: Now do the same for the word "Switzerland." First write some obvious associations such as William Tell, cuckoo clocks, bank accounts, mountains, yodeling, and so on. Next add any unusual associations that spring to mind. You may remember a holiday in Italy or France near the Swiss border. Or you may think of a Swiss friend you once knew. If anything incongruous comes to you, add it as well, even if it isn't directly connected logically to the subject of your free association of ideas.

Step 5: Pause and think about any subjects you wrote in the ovals. Do any of them remind you of something from your dream? If none do, continue adding more ovals until one does. The act of trying to remember your dream may trigger new material that comes spontaneously. It might not be anything to do with Switzerland or with eating. It could be a completely new snippet. Put this in a new oval linked from the main one and add associations to it as you did with Switzerland and food.

Step 6: If you find that one of the things you've written down does remind you of something from your dream continue to build more links from it. For example, you remember that it was cheese you were eating. Start making links around the word cheese. This could include names of cheeses, your personal associations with cheese, you may even think of things like the moon, cheesy socks, and so on. Again, one or two of your associations may bring to mind more details about the dream.

Step 7: You can continue making associations with each part of the dream for as long as you like. Your branches and notes in the ovals will gradually spread out from each other until they fill the page. Dreams are naturally very fragmented so this technique also helps you bring together the parts of dream story lines that run in different directions.

Step 8: Finally, write a summary of the dream that you have recalled. Date it and give it a title as you would for a normal journal entry.

USING DREAM MAPS TO RECALL OTHER DREAMS

The dream map technique can also be useful with dreams that have been clearly recalled. Once you've logged your dream in your journal write the title of the dream in the center of a page and draw an oval round it.

This time draw branches from it to ovals that contain other dreams that you can associate with this current dream. For example, you have the classic dream of being chased by a shadowy figure. It may remind you of dreams from childhood, perhaps from a time when you were going through a difficulty such as being bullied at school.

Give the past dream a title and draw new branches and ovals with as many details as you can remember.

You may find that dozens of dreams from the past come to mind. Some may be fairly recent and others may reach back to early childhood. You will begin to see that patterns emerge in your dreams. Dreams also have a strange way of picking up on the thread of a story that they left a long time earlier. Sometimes you have to wait many years for the next episode!

DREAM DICTIONARY

By working with dreams over many years and recalling dreams from a long time ago you may come to realize that you have another life that lives in tandem with your present waking life. This inner life has its own stories, high points, tragedies, and episodes just like your outer life. Most people associate their lives with the world outside themselves—career, family, status, possessions, and so on. A rich dream life reveals another you that is not dependent on these things. Your dream journal is the history of this inner you.

If you recall dream sequences from your past, you will notice that many themes and images return time after time. Certain symbols, metaphors, and allegories will recur that have a meaning that is uniquely yours. If you keep good records you can identify common symbols from your dreams and make them into a personal dream dictionary. This could be made as a separate book, or you can use the back section of your dream journal.

KEEPING A DREAM DICTIONARY

Step 1: As you did with the dream maps, you must break your dream down into its components. For example, suppose you dream about a blue tree being washed by the sea. In this dream are three possible entries to your dictionary section: tree, sea, and the color blue. Once you have understood the dream you can write your interpretation for the meaning of each of the symbols. Dedicate the last 26 pages of your dream diary to your dictionary; give at least one page to each letter of the alphabet. If you use a loose-leaf binder you can add new pages as your dictionary grows.

Step 2: Read through the dreams in your journal and identify any symbols you may find. Remember that every entry may reveal many symbols, such as color, imagery, places, and people. In addition you may want to list actions and scenarios such as being chased, falling, teeth falling out, or being in your childhood home.

Step 3: Make a reference to the dream titles and dates so that you can quickly cross-reference your entries.

Step 4: Give your interpretation of the meaning and include some of your personal associations with the symbols. For example, you may dream of falling. You may notice that this dream always happens when you are "falling" asleep. A drop in blood pressure may cause the dream. Alternatively, you may also notice that you dream of falling when you feel insecure or have difficult problems to sort out. The date entries you make will help you identify some of the situations in real life that trigger this common dream. The dream may also bring to mind memories of a fall you had as a child. Note everything that feels important in association with this dream metaphor. Next time you have a similar dream, half the work of the interpretation will already have been done when you analyze it.

Step 5: Leave a little space below each entry so you can add more detail the next time you have a similar dream. You will discover that your dream symbols can change their meaning as you work with them. Dreams use symbols similar to the way we use words. We string words together to create sentences that convey meaning; so; too; a dream is like a sentence of symbols. Just as words mean different things depending on their context so too do dream symbols. As has been mentioned already, we dream in symbols because that may be the way the subconscious mind talks to the conscious, or waking, mind.

Step 6: You may never really know the exact meanings of the symbols or why they come into your dreams. They are elusive and change and evolve as you work with them. However, it will help you understand them better if you also study the traditional meanings of symbols while considering your own interpretations. A symbol dictionary can give you ideas to explain things that appear in your dreams. It will show you the psychological way to understand dream symbolism as well as showing you some of the strange superstitions associated with each dream symbol.

DREAM DICTIONARY TIP

Near each dream entered in your dictionary record the date of the dream. Check if anything reminds you of things happening in your waking life. Include this under the dream dictionary entry. Use a different color pen for the notes about your waking life to make it easier to differentiate them.

The I Ching and Dream Recall

The *I Ching*, or the Book of Changes, is an ancient oracle that originated in China and has been used throughout the Far East for thousands of years. It is principally a work of guidance to help anyone seeking help and enlightenment on any subject. It has also been used to augur how to find good fortune and avoid adversity. In China it was so influential, matters of state were often decided by it and it was one of the few books not obliterated during the Cultural Revolution. Even in Japan it was and still is used extensively. For example, the decision to make the sudden attack on

Pearl Harbor in December 1941 was made only after experts had consulted the *I Ching*.

It has today caught the imagination of many Westerners and is used throughout the world.

The wisdom of the *I Ching* is older than Christianity and has been passed down through the generations since the fourth millennium BC. It is much more than a means of prediction. It is a book that offers advice how to cope with your fortune.

The central feature of the *I Ching* is the hexagram, a pattern of six horizontal lines that are read from the bottom upward. The random division of yarrow sticks, wands, or coins determine these. According to the Chinese sages who wrote the book the resulting hexagram is not a product of chance but is the touchstone that will answer the questioner's predicament. (The ancient Chinese believed that the spirits (*shên*) of the ancestors were communicating with them through the medium of chance.) Once the hexagram has been determined, it can be looked up in the text of the *I Ching* and the answer interpreted in the light of the question asked.

The philosophy of the *I Ching* is based on ancient Taoism and is also profoundly influenced by the teachings of the philosopher Confucius and by the religion of Buddhism. Taoism proposes that all pairs of opposites in nature, such as male and female, light and dark, black and white, each contain the seed of each other. They continually transform into each other, thus creating perpetual change and order within chaos. The Chinese called these two forces Yin and Yang. This polarity theory underlies most of the great religions of Asia.

Material reality is yin. Yin covers all things tangible, things that can be held. Yin is a feminine force and represents earth or matter. It is symbolized by a square, is black, and is associated with night, stillness, downward motion, the interior, winter, and the north. Yang is the intangible aspect of creation represented by heaven. Its symbol is a circle, and it is considered a masculine principle. It is white and is associated with daytime, activity, upward motion, exteriors, summer, and the south. Yin and Yang are fundamental to Chinese philosophy. They are not seen as opposite forces but as complementary, altering, and moving each other in an eternal process of change. The interaction of these two principles gives rise to all things.

In the early 1920s analytical psychologist Carl Jung met Richard Wilhelm, who had translated the *I Ching* into German. In 1923 Jung invited Wilhelm to lecture in Zurich, where he spoke on the *I Ching* at the Psychology Club. Jung was deeply impressed by what Wilhelm had to say and began an intensive study of oracle. In *Memories, Reflections, Dreams*, Jung wrote: "I would sit for hours on the ground beneath the hundred-year-old pear tree, the *I Ching* beside me, practicing the technique by referring the resultant oracles to one another in an interplay of questions and answers.

All sorts of undeniably remarkable results emerged—meaningful connections with my own thought processes which I could not explain to myself."

Jung realized that the *I Ching* was a means by which he could access the unconscious mind. The paranormal chance phenomena of the *I Ching* appeared to be "meaningful coincidences." In 1930, he first used the term synchronicity to describe an "a-causal connection between psychic states and objective events." His initial theories were influenced by a classical idea of astrology called the "objective moment." This is the basis of most fortune-telling systems and proposes that certain quality exists in a given moment of time itself. For example, whatever is done at this moment of time, has the quality of this moment of time. In other words, random events such as the dealing of Tarot cards, the position of the stars at your birth or the fall of dice or coins are influenced by the conditions of the present moment. Oracles that use these methods reflect the underlying conditions and can reveal the potential for the future.

Carl Jung understood that the *I Ching* was a means by which he could look into the underlying influences that were creating current psychological conditions. He found that the *I Ching* could be used to interpret dreams. It could also identify underlying psychological conditions and reveal what was denied or hidden. Furthermore, it was a useful tool to restore psychological equilibrium and integration.

The *I Ching* gave Jung an insight into what was happening in the unconscious of himself and his patients. In his foreword to the *I Ching* Jung wrote: "The method of the *I Ching* does indeed take into account the hidden individual quality in things and men, and in one's own unconscious self as well."

Clearly the *I Ching* can be used to help interpret dreams, but it can also be used to help you get in touch with your inner self so that forgotten dreams can be remembered.

Example: Using the *I Ching* for dream recall

It is customary to consult the *I Ching* for its permission and comments before writing about it. Jung did a similar exercise when he prepared the original foreword. In Jung's case the *I Ching* had compared itself to a cauldron (*ting*)–a ritual vessel containing cooked food. Here the food is understood to be spiritual nourishment. This is clearly an apt metaphor for the *I Ching*, which provides spiritual nourishment and wisdom to many people.

I asked for its opinion how it should be used as a means of recalling dreams and was given hexagram 37, *The Family (Chia Jên)*. At first this made no sense to me, then part way through my second reading I remembered my dream from the previous night. The *I Ching* was demonstrating dream recall by example.

That morning I had overslept and had no time to write my dreams in my diary. I knew I had had a dream but I could only recall a few snippets. As soon as I got up I rushed straight into my home office to make a few important telephone calls. In my haste I had completely forgotten my dream.

Later that day when I cast the hexagram of *The Family* it brought the dream memory back. I had dreamt about being in a graveyard surrounded by family crypts. One was of famous people, one was of rich people, and the last, which I had to clear weeds to find, was titled "ordinary folk." I had a bunch of flowers and decided to lay them on the family crypt of "ordinary folk."

This strange dream made sense. It symbolized my work as a spiritualist medium. I have given consultations to the rich and famous but it is the consultations for "ordinary folk" that are spiritually the most important. These are the readings that unite parents with their dead children, husbands, and wives and bring together loved ones and family across the veil of death. Correct mediumship proves that families are forever and that love is eternal and will never die.

Clearly, the *I Ching* had helped me remember an important dream about families that highlighted the values that need to be remembered with my spiritual work.

I CHING EXPERIMENT

The *I Ching* does not always give you the answer you expect. It has been said of the *I Ching* that it has a personality of its own and even a sense of humor. Jung advised that the *I Ching* be approached with the reverence of a wise sage.

Step 1: The *I Ching* will answer your question in accordance with the way the question is phrased and its text must be regarded as though the book were the speaking person. You may ask it: "Help me remember the dream I had last night" and you will get clues and prompts to help you recover lost dream memories.

Step 2: Cast the hexagram and read the text. To do this you will of course need a copy of the *I Ching*. There is not space here to describe how to cast the *I Ching* or to reproduce the 64 hexagrams with their many moving lines.

Step 3: Read the text through without trying to relate it to your life or to the dreams you've had. This relaxed state of mind will allow the imagery of the *I Ching* to sink into your unconscious and draw information to you. You may find that the title of the hexagram, the qualities of the trigrams, the characters, scenarios, and images from the text act as direct clues that trigger spontaneous recall. Don't worry too much about what the text means; be concerned about the images that it provokes.

Step 4: If a dream memory is not triggered with the first reading read the text again but this time think about the psychological qualities that the hexagram describes. For example hexagram 28, *The Preponderance of the Great*, can show someone who is under pressure. Was your dream about being under pressure? Hexagram 5, *Waiting*, talks about nourishment. Perhaps your dream contained images of food or involved a situation or where you were waiting for something? Hexagram 14, *Possession on Great Measure*, may refer to dreams about finding treasure, and hexagram 27, *The Corners of the Mouth*, may refer to the common dream of teeth falling out. The hexagram 29, *The Abysmal*, could trigger the recall of a dream about falling and hexagram 15, *Modesty*, may make indicate Freud's favorite dream: being naked in public!

Step 5: The hexagrams of the *I Ching* contain many archetypal images and potent symbols that arise from the unconscious. The mythical and magical qualities of the *I Ching* are conducive to dream recall. However there are no set rules about which hexagram relates to which dream. The symbols within the book are flexible. They are a mirror to your unconscious mind.

Step 6: If you recall a dream, write it in your dream diary. Also include the hexagram and the main images that prompted the recall. If you get the same hexagram again when you next do this technique, you may find that the oracle is pointing to a recurring dream or an ongoing sequence of dreams. Your records will help you with dream recall in the future.

Step 7: If you fail to remember a dream using this technique, note the hexagram in your dream diary anyway. The hexagram will reveal information about your inner life, which is one of the main functions of dreams. Later, you can return to the hexagrams you cast to re-evaluate your original interpretation. If you cannot discover any immediate relevance in a given response, you may be limited by your expectations. Later the hexagram may make sense in the light of future events and future dreams.

Step 8: If you recall a dream using this technique try casting another hexagram to interpret the dream. The *I Ching* can give remarkable insight into the psychological influences that are responsible for the inception of your dream.

For some people the spirit of the *I Ching* is clear and for others it may convey nothing. Jung found that the Western mind tends to shut out intuitive prompts because reason and the intellect rule most of us. However, an open-minded attitude toward oracles such as the *I Ching* can re-establish a rapport with the intuitive self and can bring great benefit to the personality. Recognizing your intuitive side as well as your intellectual side can help you become a more stable and well-rounded individual.

Tarot Cards and other oracles

Most oracles can be used to access the unconscious and help you recall dreams. Tarot cards are particularly rich in the archetypal symbolism that emerges from the world of dreams. Even if you have no idea of the traditional meanings of the cards they can reveal a great deal about what's happening in your unconscious. For example, if you randomly draw a card while asking about your dream, the pictures on the cards can act as triggers to help you access this knowledge.

Traditional oracles are rich in dream symbolism. Just as you used the *I Ching*, so too you could easily adapt oracles such as runes, dice, cards, sand reading, and so on. Instead of asking questions about your life, ask instead about your dreams. They will help you recall forgotten dreams as well as helping you with the task of interpreting the dreams you do recall.

Long before science took an interest in the study of dreams, mystics were using dreams to foretell the future, diagnose illness, and give counseling and guidance. In particular, dreams have been revered by seers and prophets as messages from God. Psychics and Spiritualists have seen them as ways to access the past, future, and the spheres of the spirits and angels. Dreams have been remembered and interpreted since the dawn of consciousness, but perhaps the man who did most to secure mystical dreams a place in the modern age was the American prophet Edgar Cayce.

Edgar Cayce

Edgar Cayce was born in Kentucky in 1877. He was a humble man with a Presbyterian background who ran a small photography business for most of his life. What singled him out from ordinary individuals was what happened when he went to sleep. He was known as "the sleeping prophet." While asleep (it was actually a trancelike state) he would make predictions and give medical treatments. When he awoke he had no recollection--or even understanding--of what he had said.

During his life Cayce gave over 14,000 "readings" as he called them. These included herbal cures, correct diagnosis and treatments for patients who were not even present at the consultation, and many predictions about the future of mankind. For example, in April 1929, a stockbroker consulted him about a dream, and the sleeping Cayce declared that there would be panic on Wall Street and around the world. He said that prices would fluctuate over a period of six months and then collapse. On Friday, October 29, 1929, Wall Street crashed bringing chaos in its wake and the great Depression.

In June 1931, Cayce spoke about the coming of the Second World War. He also foresaw the end of Communism in Russia which would result in an alliance between Russia and the U.S.A. that would be the "hope of the world." He further predicted the Christianization of Red China, massive earthquakes, the sliding of much of Japan into the sea, the destruction of most of Los Angeles, San Francisco, and New York and the tilting of the earth's rotational axis with a drastic reversal of global climates.

Perhaps it would have been better if Cayce's dreams had remained forgotten!

Cayce's theories about dreams were very different from those of Freud and Jung. Cayce believed dreaming to be the body's way of "self edification," a term he used to describe the building up of the mental, spiritual, and physical well-being of the individual.

Dreams are a form of spiritual growth that quicken the dreamer to his/her human potential. A good night's sleep resulted in a better person who had more mature values and creative thinking. A good night's sleep developed in a person proper conduct and thinking.

According to Cayce, dreams have five different levels: the body level, subconscious level, level of consciousness, level of super-conscious, and the level of the soul. Dreams can help to bring health and insight into each of these parts. For example, they could present messages about the body and call for aid during illness.

Cayce believed that in order to interpret dreams correctly it is first necessary to study oneself thoroughly. The primary purpose of dreams is either to solve problems and adapt to external affairs or to alert the dreamer to new potential. The first step is to determine whether the dream is about problems or potential.

The next step is to make an inventory. It is important to know your conscious and subconscious hopes and fears. You must also be aware of your future plans, goals, interests, opinions, and decisions. Similarly, you must be honest with yourself about your hidden fears, longings, dependencies, and denials. Know too the cycles, needs, habits, and stresses of the body. Only when you are aware of all these things can you interpret your dreams satisfactorily.

Dreams function on all five levels. If you know yourself, you can more easily make the decisions that help you better yourself physically, subconsciously, consciously, super-consciously, and at the level of the soul.

Cayce's Dream Recall Methods

Cayce believed that all normal people--people without severe brain damage--dream but have problems remembering their dreams. He coached many "non-dreamers" how to recall their dreams without difficulty. However he always advised that they must first be prepared to confront whatever dreams revealed. Furthermore they had to be willing to apply the dream revelations to their life.

People who wanted to recall their dreams had to be ready to make changes to their life and to themselves. Cayce considered this the key to dream recall.

Practical methods included dream incubation, such as telling oneself, just before dropping to sleep, to remember a dream. Some people were encouraged to stimulate dreams by reading and talking about them, others were instructed to pray for dream guidance. Different methods of dream recall suit people of differing temperaments and inclinations.

Cayce also believed that the body had a role in remembering dreams, that retaining the same position on awakening and allowing oneself to drift in and out of sleep could help a dream be revealed. He stressed the importance of getting enough rest. He also encouraged his students to talk about and record their dreams. He spoke of the need for an "inquiring mind." He explained that even a fragment of a dream could be the key that unlocked the whole dream. If a fragment could be recalled, Cayce would sometimes give a prompt using clairvoyance to remind the sitter of the missing memories.

Cayce also spoke about what happened to dreams that were not recalled. According to him, many dreams exist to advance the dreamer's spiritual growth but others are just worries, dreams about food or bodily processes, or dreams to help dreamer continue sleeping. Some dreams are clearly not that important. Cayce also said that dreams of the sick or damaged body are not worth recalling and interpreting. However, he insisted that dreams are a natural aid by which the personality and body regulate themselves and improve the dreamer's situation. Significant dreams will repeat and appear in different forms and continue to convey the same message until the dreamer remembers them.

For Cayce, dreams were not something odd and removed from everyday life. Just as dreams can reveal the future, so can a waking hunch. Dreams give important insights into and highlight weaknesses but this same information can be discovered through introspection. Perhaps the most important thing Cayce had to say about dreams, and something he constantly emphasized, was that dreams are recalled so they can be used. It is important to act on the dreams you recall. If you do this you will increase your self-knowledge and enhance the quality of your daily living.

4 WORKING WITH YOUR DREAMS

Learn from your dreams what you lack
W H Auden (1907-73)
English poet and playwright

If you've used the techniques already shown, you should now have many dreams to work with. In fact, you may have too many! Once you get the knack of dream recall you remember so many dreams, you may feel swamped. You must decide which ones are the most important ones you have remembered. In this section, you'll work with your most important dreams to discover what they are trying to tell you about yourself.

You may have noticed that certain themes recur in your dreams. For example, I occasionally dream about missing the train, running out of paper for my computer printer, or of being unprepared for an important talk. These are common anxiety dreams that can arise when I feel under pressure. This type of dream contains metaphors, allegories, and symbols that express my feelings of being unprepared. I often have them if I am struggling to meet a publisher's deadline!

Identify the dreams you have had that share a common theme. Dreams sometimes expand on themes from the previous night's dreams and present similar material in a different way. In the example I cited of my own dreams, all the dreams have the same theme presented in different ways. They all highlight my feelings about being unprepared and my anxiety about not being able to complete the job I have to do. Similar dreams could include rushing to get the bus but missing it or taking an examination and realizing that you do not know the subject matter.

Similar emotional themes can be presented in many different ways. Once you recognize the emotional theme of the dream, it is important to make changes in your life and to act on what your unconscious is telling you. Put the dream's advice into practice. In my case, I took a day off and ignored the panic deadline. When I returned to the job at hand, I felt refreshed and able to cope. The result was that I could complete the job with twice the efficiency I would have had if I had continued to be anxious. The dream pointed out the problem and I acted upon it.

Preparation

Go through your dream diary and decide which types of dreams have been occurring the most. They may be sexual dreams, anxiety dreams, dreams about childhood, and so on. Perhaps you have been dreaming about a specific person or place. Recurring dreams are important because they show inner conflicts or difficulties that you have not resolved. They may point to problems you are experiencing now or to unresolved problems from long ago. Many recurring dreams and nightmares deal with the issues you refuse to face.

Early dream interpreters

In the fifth century BC, Greek philosopher Heraclitus suggested that a person's dreams were created by his own mind. This may seem obvious but at the time this was a revolutionary idea. Other philosophers believed that outside forces were responsible for dreams. They were given to men by the gods, angels, or the spirits. Aristotle took the idea a stage further and in *Parva naturalia* suggested that dreams were in fact a recollection of the day's events. He attributed dreams to sensory impressions from "external objects…pauses within the body…eddies…of sensory movement often remaining like they were when they first started, but often too broken into other forms by collision with obstacles." Aristotle also proposed that dreams can reflect a person's health and may warn of the onset of illness or may give remedies and cures.

The first comprehensive book on the interpretation of dreams was the *Oneirocriticon* by the Roman writer Artemidorus. (AD 150). This five-volume work proposed that dreams were unique to the dreamer. Artemidorus argued that the person's occupation, social status, and health would influence the dream. The dream would represent these aspects of the person's life by means of symbols.

A second version of the books was written by Astrampsychus, another Roman writer. Unfortunately, instead of helping the dreamer to see the true psychological meaning of the symbols *Oneirocriticon* version two gave specific meanings to each category of dream. Some of the interpretations are ridiculous. For example, it stated "To wear a purple robe threatens a long disease," and "To hold or eat eggs symbolizes vexation."

Although the ancients may not have understood the causes or psychological significance of dreams, they nevertheless knew that dreams were important. As messages from the gods, they could be used to guide our lives and give answers to problems that worried us. Many ancient texts are full of references to dreams. The Egyptians, Greeks, Romans, Jews, and Christians were all fascinated by dreams and based many of their personal, religious and political decisions upon what their symbols revealed. Dream interpretation was a skilled and revered art.

When working with your dreams, it is important to get in the right frame of mind. It is best to be cheerful, open-minded, and prepared to accept what you discover about yourself. It is wise to be resolved that you will act on what you discover. If you recognize a fault in yourself, you may want to correct it. Interpreting your dreams will require you to make changes in your life and in your attitude toward others. And most importantly, you will feel the urge to make changes in yourself.

Inevitably, you will be dealing with some of your most sensitive points and may unearth things about yourself you would prefer not to know. Sometimes working with dreams can be difficult. We all have petty thoughts and infantile attitudes hidden behind the mask we show the world. None of us are the people we would like to think we are. Nobody is faultless. Some of your thoughts and motives may not be wholesome. We all harbor hidden resentments, jealousies, insecurities, and so on. Bringing them to the light of day unmasks hidden fears and loosens the grip they have at an unconscious level. They will then no longer be terrifying. Finally by resolving inner strife and integrating the dark side, it is possible to become much happier and more peaceful within.

Dream Symbols

Many of the dream guide books and dictionaries that you buy today are based on old superstitions. The specific interpretations for each dream are all but useless and say very little about the true meanings of dreams. Dream dictionaries written from a psychological standpoint can be a useful guide to help you unravel symbols you find difficult. However, dictionaries that say things such as "To dream of being scratched by a black cat signifies that an enemy will steal your business" are utter nonsense. Wacky things are fun but not much use as a tool to help you interpret dreams.

You need to know the psychological meaning of a dream and not base your interpretation on the nonsensical arbitrary interpretations of superstition. But most important are your own personal associations and feelings connected with the symbols of the dream. For example, if you are a cat lover a cat may represent companionship, perhaps with a wild streak of independence. For another person a cat may be associated with witches or the incarnations of the Egyptian souls of the dead. Common interpretations for cats are treachery and deceit.

Every dream you have is unique to you. Dreams describe your innermost self. They reveal the truth about you. Carl Jung put it succinctly when he said that a dream "shows inner truth and reality...as it really is: not as I conjecture it to be, and not as (the dreamer) would like it to be, but as it is."

Symbolism is a living thing that changes and develops within society and for the individual. Many of the superstitions to be found in dream dictionaries are thousands of years old. Their meanings may no longer be relevant to modern times and they may mean something completely different. If you feel that the meaning in a dream book is wrong for you-- even in dream books by me!--examine exactly what the dream object means for your life and go with that interpretation. There are no "oven- ready" answers to the meanings of dreams. The best way to understand them is simply to trust your instincts.

Many psychological interpretations of dreams are also dubious. For example, few people today believe that Freud was right in presuming that so much of the symbolism of dreams is sexual. Clearly some of it is, and Freud made some tremendously important observations about the forces that are at work below the surface of consciousness. However, Freudian theories, like all psychology and psychological theories, are just that: theories. Theories come in and out of fashion. We still have no clear picture what dreams do or what they mean, if anything at all. The truth is, only you can decide what the real meaning of your dream is. After all, your dreams, like your thoughts, are yours.

Common Dreams

Many dream images are personal: the figure of a friend; an object you once owned with particular associations, the recollection of a holiday, or a house where you once lived. To understand the meaning of most dreams you need to decipher the complex associations that you have with the many symbols that occur. However, there are also many dream symbols and themes that most people have in common. For example, have you ever dreamed of being chased? This is a metaphor for insecurity. You may feel that circumstances are closing in on you and you are at the mercy of feelings that are out of control. This type of common dream is urging you to stop running away from your problems and to face up to something. You may be attempting to escape from something about yourself you don't like. Perhaps you've done something and you want to escape the feelings of guilt or shame. Alternatively, you may be running from something that worries you in your life. For example, children who have this dream may be worried about being bullied at school.

There are many such common dreams. Flying is a common dream and usually denotes a release of tension. You may dream of being nude in public, showing that you may have sexual inhibitions or a fear of having something about you or your life exposed. You may dream of finding treasure, or dream of sex, accidents, snakes, or strange buildings. You will find that a great many people have had the same or similar dreams. Most dreams are metaphors and symbols for your emotional states of mind.

Dreams often contain archetypal images that are found in religious and mythical symbolism all over the world. Dreams use these collective symbols as an artist uses color. However, your dream paints pictures based on your unique experience.

Dream Interpretation

It is generally agreed that dreams are the voice of the unconscious talking to you in the language of metaphor, allegory, and symbolism. They are rarely what they seem to be and may sometimes appear to have nothing to do with your life now. However, once you observe the emotions, moods, and symbolism of your dream you will find that they are expressing things about you and your situation that are relevant to your life at the moment. They are there to help you.

EXPERIMENT Interpreting a dream

Objective: In this experiment, you will interpret one of dreams you have entered in your dream diary.

Step 1: Chose a dream that is recent and that follows a similar theme as other dreams you've been having. In your dream diary, you will have written this dream on the left. You will now write your interpretation in the right- hand column.

Step 2: EXAMINE YOUR FEELINGS At the top of the right-hand side of the page write down the feelings the dream invokes. For example, is it a happy or sad dream? Perhaps the dream makes you feel frightened, worried, or joyous and exhilarated. If the dream contains a mixture of emotions, write all of them down. Clearly identifying the emotions the dream contains helps you see the part of your life the dream is talking about.

When did you last feel the same feelings in your waking life? If you felt fear, think about what things have frightened you lately. It may not necessarily be something tangible. You may be frightened by the implication of what someone has said to you or you may have hidden fears about a potential situation. Similarly, if you have good feelings think about the time you last felt these feelings. Perhaps they represent the way you wish you were feeling now? Often dreams will compensate for emotions that cannot be expressed in general life. Most people do not spontaneously express extreme emotions like anger or respond actively to every sexual urge. In life we have to control ourselves but in dreams the emotions run free.

Write down the emotions in your diary and also the part of your life you feel they express. For example, you may write: "Anger? Fear? Relationship worries? Injustice at work?" As soon as you link the feelings from your dream with something recognizable in your life, the dream may spontaneously make sense. All of a sudden, it will click. "Aha! So that's what it's talking about." you say.

If you feel sufficiently relaxed about working with your dreams you may find that the meaning will become clear as soon as you start writing. If it does, just go with the flow and write down whatever meaning becomes immediately apparent. Usually your first thoughts about a dream's meaning are the right ones.

Step 3: ESTABLISH AN OVERVIEW OF THE CONTENT

Dreams describe your problems in story form. They say things such as: "My frustration with this situation feels just like walking through a muddy field," or "I feel that if my emotions get out of control it will be just like having a car accident," or "I feel so unprepared for my presentation it's like turning up for a public meeting without my notes." Ask yourself if your dream is an allegory that represents something that has been happening to you in real life. Write down your observations in your dream diary. At this stage, take an overview rather than getting tied down with specific details.

In the following steps you should make detailed notes in the column on the right and highlight any areas of the original dream that you feel are especially significant. You may also wish to make sketches, mind maps, or use various colored pencils to help you come to your conclusions.

Step 4: CONSIDER THE DREAMSCAPE

The landscape you see in your dream can also express your innermost thoughts. For example, mountains can represent the lofty planes of consciousness. It is the realm of the higher self, the part of you that has higher, transcendent knowledge. Dreaming of being at the top of a mountain may show how you now feel that you have risen above the common routines of life and achieved something with spiritual meaning. On a more mundane level, climbing a mountain may symbolize your sense of achievement and the arduous effort needed for a long-term undertaking. You are on the slippery slope of success and have the self-determination to reach the summit.

Similarly, a plain may symbolize feelings of loneliness or an easy pathway ahead. A valley may show that your choices are limited. A journey through a valley sometimes symbolizes the transition from one set of circumstances to another.

Look to see if you noted in your dream diary anything about the environment you saw in the dream. Interpret this as a symbol of the way you feel or as an expression of what you feel about the course of your life at the moment.

Buildings and houses will also express aspects of yourself The upstairs can represent your conscious mind and the lower floors and cellar, your hidden self. The cramped feeling of the cellar can indicate frustration and a need to expand your activities or thinking. Decayed or crumbling buildings may indicate that your self-image has suffered. Different parts of a house may symbolize different times. For example, modern rooms may represent the conscious mind whereas the oldest areas may represent the ancient mind, the unconscious. Also, the condition of the building may express how you feel about yourself. Sometimes decayed buildings are the prelude to the onset of an illness.

Your moods and feelings may also be described by the weather that occurs in your dream. For example, stormy skies may show arguments and anger; sunshine may show happiness, rain may show release from tension, and snow may indicate that your emotions are frozen.

Step 5: OBSERVE COLORS AND FEELINGS. What do the colors in your dream tell you about your feelings? Color can evoke strong emotional responses, and the colors in dreams can reveal a great deal about your emotional state. Psychologists use color tests to judge the emotional condition of their patients. However color meanings can vary from individual to individual, and you may have your own personal associations with a particular color. Red represents passion and sexuality. It can also represent anger or blood, the color of the life force. Yellow is often associated with artistic inspiration. Yellow is sometimes considered the color of the coward. Green is the color of nature and brings new life and hope. Its negative association is with jealousy. Blue is the spiritual color. It is claimed to be the color that healers have in their auric field. Blue brings harmony and, like the sky, implies freedom. And of course, it can sometimes represent depression when we get the blues. Black is usually a color associated with depression. Time to get rid of those black thoughts. It may also indicate unconsciousness, whereas white is usually a symbol of purity.

Step 6: WHO IS IN YOUR DREAM? If you dream of people you know, it may be your unconscious making you aware of qualities and feelings you desire. The feelings that your interaction with them gives you will be those you are becoming aware of in real life. If you dream of people you do not know, this may be a way of confronting aspects of yourself. Ask yourself what the dream says about the hidden aspects of you. Do you like the person in the dream? What does this person mean to you? Often the people and characters who appear in dreams represent aspects of you or your life.

Most of the people we dream about represent aspects of ourselves. Supposing you perceive your mother as bossy and you dream about her, your dream may be saying you're getting too bossy, just like your mother.

Step 6: WHAT'S WHAT The people, animals, and objects that occur in your dreams are symbols that usually comment on your feelings. For example, suppose you dream about wiping your muddy boots on a doormat. Such a dream may indicate how you treat other people. You walk all over them and rub in the dirt! The dream could also represent the way you feel others mistreat you. You could be the doormat who is being walked over. It is important to understand that you have to work your way around every symbol to come to a meaningful interpretation. Carl Jung wrote: "Even if one has great experience in these matters, one is again obliged, before each dream, to admit one's ignorance and, renouncing all preconceived ideas, to prepare for something entirely unexpected."

You may also find that some of your dreams contain animals. Animals signify the primal, instinctive, and sometimes base desires. Your dream may be drawing your attention to an aspect of your nature that you undervalue or part of yourself that you repress. Try to get in touch with the "natural" you. Be more spontaneous and less rational. Within everyone is a deep instinctive energy that has a transforming power. Animals may also express certain qualities: For example, a dog may represent devotion, a cat may represent the intuition, a tiger may represent fear, and a pig may symbolize gluttony and bad behavior. Sometimes animals can represent other people, i.e. we often describe people with animal images: sly as a fox, slippery as a fish, a lying snake, strong as an ox, etc.

Step 7: LOOK AT THE SPECIFIC DETAILS Once you have established a general meaning for your dream you can look at the specific details to see if they can reveal more information about the meaning of the dream. For example, dreams often contain puns. I once dreamed of using a pencil and when I unraveled the dream I realized that it was about my friend Mark. Most of the things found in dreams are symbols specifically for you. Your dream will be drawing comparisons and will remind you of many things from your own life. It may be saying that "you feel happy *just like* the day you got married, or you need a break *just like* your holiday in Florida, or the pressure you feel is *just like* the day you took your exams at school."

Step 8: LOOK BACK By considering the above aspects of your dream you will gradually unravel its mystery and come to a clearer understanding of what your dream is saying abort you and your life. Having kept scrupulous dream records you also have many other dreams you can work with. You may want to note the main symbols of your dream in the back of your dream diary to form a simple dream dictionary. This will also help you identify other dreams that have a similar theme or have the same symbols. Once you have enjoyed deciphering your initial dreams you will soon be looking forward to the sequels.

Interpreting dreams from a long time ago

You may find it useful to practice your interpretation skills by working with memorable dreams from the past. Try recalling your worst nightmare. Note the details in your dream diary and give an approximate date or year when it occurred. What is it that frightened you? Can you now relate these fears to problems you were experiencing at that time?

Analyze the dream using the techniques you've learned so far and try to discover what it was that was troubling you. In retrospect, it is easier to see through worries you had then now that you're free of them. If the nightmare still recurs you will need to work with the dream to discover what it is that still calls for your attention. There may be things about yourself or your life that you don't want to know and have pushed into the unconscious. The nightmare is telling you that you need to pay attention to what the unconscious has to say. It wants to help you establish inner harmony and well being.

Similarly, work with the best dreams you remember. Again, write down in your dream diary what you can recall about these dreams. Collect dreams the way people collect butterflies. Use your interpretation techniques to find out what your dream was telling you about your feelings at that time. Pleasurable dreams may be showing you your hopes and ambitions. Have you fulfilled these yet, or are there still hopes and wishes you have not achieved? Dreams are an important way to get to know what you really want out of life.

PUTTING YOUR DREAMS TO GOOD USE

Imagine what it would be like if you could harness the power of dreams and use them to solve your creative and intellectual problems. Dreams are a powerful creative tool. They reflect your emotions, feelings, anxieties, and problems but also offer solutions how to solve them. Dreams are a creative experience providing solutions to problems and occasionally giving brilliant ideas that might never have occurred in waking life.

Many creative people have been helped by dreams. For example, the story of *Alice in Wonderland* came to author Lewis Carroll in a dream that occurred during a period of sickness. Similarly, the English poet Samuel Taylor Coleridge claimed that he had written the poem Kubla Khan as the result of a dream. He fell asleep after reading about the Mongol conqueror. When he awoke, he remembered and wrote a fully developed poem which he had composed while dreaming. Also, novelist Robert Louis Stevenson said that "little people" in his dreams developed much of his writing. He specifically cited the story of Dr. Jekyll and Mr. Hyde, claiming it was inspired by a dream. Likewise Jules Verne and Charles Dickens were inspired by dreams, and the characters in Jane Eyre were spun from the dreams of Charlotte Brontë.

Remarkable scientific discoveries have also been made because of dreams. German chemist A. Kekulé von Stradonitz attributed his interpretation of the ring structure of the benzene molecule to his dream of a snake with its tail in its mouth, a discovery that launched the German synthetic-dye industry. Similarly, German physiologist Otto Loewi attributed to a dream inspiration for an experiment with a frog's nerve that helped him win the Nobel Prize.

In many cases, solutions given by dreams come after considerable time spent thinking about a problem. Dreams take over where the conscious mind leaves off. Dreams can sometimes cut to the heart of an issue and offer simple answers to complex problems. There are times when a dream presents a solution to a problem when you don't have all the facts at hand. It could be that some dreams access information by paranormal means. For example, naturalist Louis Agassiz dreamed of the complete form of a fossil fish that was mostly hidden within a stone slab. Stumped by the faint traces on the surface, Agassiz dreamed of and forgot the shape for two nights running. His third dream gave him the answer: He drew the dream fish while half awake. The fossil he chiseled from the stone slab the following day matched his drawing exactly.

As was observed in the first section of this book, the ancient Greeks slept in temples so the gods would give them solutions to problems in dreams. And while you might not expect a visitation from the gods, you can still use similar techniques to ask your unconscious to provide answers to questions.

EXPERIMENT: *Using dreams to solve problems*

OBJECTIVE: To program your inner computer to solve your emotional, creative, or intellectual problems.

Step 1: Clarify the problem. You need to be clear in your mind the exact nature of the problem you want to solve. You may have many troubles work, money, exams, or may just be stumped for a creative idea. Just before you go to sleep, write your question at the top of a page in your dream diary. Keep it clear and simple, i.e. "Should I change my job?" "What is the best way to patch up my relationship?" "How should I go about refurbishing the living room?" The act of writing the question will encourage the subconscious mind to go to work on your problem.

Step2: As you go to sleep run through the problem in your mind. Don't just think about the question in words, use pictures as well. For example, if you are worried about your job, picture yourself at work. Imagine talking about your problems with your colleagues. Imagine the sounds and smells of the office. And most important, be positive. Avoid gloomy thoughts; you don't want to go to sleep feeling depressed.

Step 3: Once you know that the information has seeped into your unconscious let go of the problem. Forget about it. Reassure yourself that you are doing the best you can to solve it. The subconscious is going to give you a dream that will wipe away all your troubles. Believe in what you are doing. Have faith in the power of your dreams.

Step 4: Your dreams will now do the rest. By thinking about the problem in an unattached way, you have given it to the subconscious. As you relax and enjoy a good night's sleep, your subconscious will be busy at work solving your problems. This is what it does anyway, but in this instance you are taking conscious control and using your sleep more efficiently. Normally the subconscious presents answers in a hit-or-miss way. This time you will be prepared to catch what it throws at you.

Step 5: In the morning write your dream in your dream diary. Telling yourself that you are going to dream will increase the likelihood that you will. Now interpret your dream as you did in the last experiment. What does the symbolism reveal about your situation?

Remember that dreams do not always give obvious answers. Sometimes they address a problem in an oblique way. For example, suppose you asked a question about work and dream that you arrived at a business function dressed only your underwear. Clearly, this is not something you should do (although the idea could be fun to imagine). The dream may be showing you that you feel vulnerable, exposed, and intimidated. The dream has pointed out that you are perhaps not self-assured enough to take on the corporate monster. Maybe you should wait until you feel more confident and prepared. Perhaps someone will expose a flaw in your strategy.

Use your dreams to help you improve yourself. If you dream of something negative, take the opposite attitude in real life. For example, suppose you ask about a relationship and you then dream about being beaten up by the school bully. The dream may illustrate that you feel dominated in your relationship. Clearly, you feel the need to develop a more assertive attitude. Make a point of behaving in the opposite way. Throughout the day focus on being more assertive. Write yourself a note and carry it with you: "Be assertive". Practice the dream's advice all day. If you do this, you will open new doors to self-confidence.

5 LUCID DREAMING TECHNIQUES

I can never decide whether my dreams are the result of my thoughts, or my thoughts the result of my dreams.
D H Lawrence (1885-1930)
English novelist

For most people dreams are a vaguely remembered experience. They are something that happened during sleep but are forgotten within moments of awakening. Most people don't realize they've been dreaming until after they have awakened and the dream has come to an end. Dreams are muddled, fuzzy, and infuriatingly hard to recall. But what if it you were able to experience dreams with the same lucidity as in normal waking consciousness? What if dreaming could be just like being wide-awake? Suppose you could wake up in a dream and experience and remember it in the same way you experience daytime events?

You may already have had one such dream. Perhaps you have "awakened" in a dream and realized you were dreaming. When it first happened to me, I dreamed of waking up, getting out of bed, and starting my usual morning routine. As I brushed my teeth, I realized I was dreaming. At that point I panicked because reality was somehow wrong. I then actually woke up. For a long time I lay in bed, unsure whether to get up or not. The dream had been so real, it was hard to know whether I was now dreaming or not.

Have you ever been dreaming, then, part way through, realized it was only a dream? Perhaps you interrupted a nightmare and realized you could stop being frightened. Dreams in which you "wake up" while the dream is taking place can become extraordinarily vivid and are believed by many societies to be especially significant. Some Native North American tribes believe it's possible to overcome many problems by using these special dreams.

Many people have the recurring dream of being chased by a shadowy figure or vicious animal. If you "wake up" in a dream such as this, according to the Native Americans, turn around to your attacker and wrestle him to the ground. In this way you will overcome your greatest fears and can become a great warrior. Similarly, if you learn to "wake up" in your dreams, you can overcome the fears that pursue you in modern life. Once challenged, such forces lose their power. There is nothing to fear for the dreamer realizes he is dreaming and has chosen to confront his inner fears. Facing these inner demons lessens the terror they are able to exert on you. In addition, this technique creates positive psychological energy that helps you to take control of your situation and state of mind.

LUCID DREAMS

In 1913 the Dutchman van Eeden called these dreams "lucid dreams" and recognized that they were not only extraordinarily vivid but could be controlled. It has been reported that 73 percent of the population have had at least one lucid dream, and lucid dreaming comes naturally to between 5 and 10 percent.

Lucid dreams can be remembered with remarkable accuracy because they are similar to normal awareness. They are so close to normal waking experience and are usually free of the irrationality and disjointed narrative of ordinary dreams. The dreamer is as conscious as in normal life and can think and remember as if wide-awake. It may appear that there is no difference between being awake and being asleep.

Awareness that the experience that seems so real is in fact a "lucid dream" occurs abruptly when the dreamer notices something unusual, inaccurate, or illogical that is happening in the dream. Something about the scenery, people, or events alerts you to the fact that you are dreaming. With this realization comes a surge of excitement and a strange feeling of higher consciousness. Sometimes the initial reaction is frightening because you are in such an unfamiliar state of awareness. Don't panic, relax, and go with the flow. You will soon learn to enjoy it. The inner world can appear more real than reality with impossibly vivid colors and intricate patterns and form. This experience may be very similar to the mescaline-induced states described by Aldous Huxley in the *Doors of Perception*: "The typical mescaline or lysergic acid experience begins with perceptions of colored, moving, living geometrical forms. In time, pure geometry becomes concrete, and the visionary perceives, not patterns, but patterned things, such as carpets, carvings, mosaics. These give place to vast and complicated buildings, in the midst of landscapes, which change continuously, passing from richness to more intensity colored richness, from grandeur to deepening grandeur."

Perhaps the most remarkable thing about lucid dreams is the dreamer's ability to control dream events like a director directing a film. The dreamer can decide where to go and what to do and can change his dream at will. Despite this, the dreamer never has complete control over the dream state. Uncontrolled events still take place and lucidity can slip in and out of ordinary dreaming. If you succeed at having a lucid dream after following the instructions later, be prepared for some surprises.

Lucid dreams have been described for centuries but are only recently being taken seriously by today's dream researchers. Freud, Adler, and Jung, although aware of them, virtually ignored them in their theories. Yet references to lucid dreaming are found in the writings of Aristotle. Saint Augustine records a lucid dream of his friend Gennadius, and Saint Thomas Aquinas also writes about them.

One of the first systematic studies of lucid dreams was made by the ancient yogis of Tibet who are well known for their extraordinary psychic, physical, and mental abilities. According to the esteemed Oxford scholar Evans-Wentz, who edited "Tibetan Yoga and Secret Doctrines," the Tibetan adepts mastered the lucid dream state. "The *yogin* learns by actual experience, resulting from psychic experimentation, that the character of any dream can be changed or transformed by willing that it shall be."

DREAM DOPPELGANGERS

Many esoteric traditions claim that seizing the initiative in dreams allows the dreamer to perform seemingly impossible things, For example, Hindu mystics claim it is possible to use dreams to bi-locate. In other words, they can appear in two places as the same time. This is an ancient tradition that many advanced yogis, and holy men and women still practice today. Once they achieve a state of lucid dreaming they visualize a location or person to visit, then by the power of dream control can appear visible to others, not just as a hazy phantom, but solid and real. Examples of this are found in the stories of the guru Yogananda as well as in the books about the secret teachings of Tibet by authors such as Alexandra David-Neel.

My own guru, Sathya Sai Baba, first called my wife Jane and me to India through lucid dreams. He appeared to both of us in dreams and also to our daughter Danielle, then 7, who claims she saw him standing in the hallway at the top of the stairs beside her room. She is adamant that he was physically present!

One dream I had about Sai Baba saw me talking to him in my home office where I write my books. It was a wonderful feeling. He hugged me and we both laughed. Partway through the dream, I said "My God, this is not a dream. This is completely real!" What I was experiencing was as real as waking consciousness. I was completely aware. It was a remarkable experience.

Sai Baba continued by telling me all about my life and what I should be doing with it. Suddenly everything seemed so simple. As I looked at him, I could see the center of his forehead open up and "thoughts" stream from him like waves of multi-colored lights. Now we were talking without language. Realizing the importance of what I was experiencing and how far removed it was from my ordinary life, I said "Oh, no, I will never remember any of this! It is all a dream and dreams fade away."

Sai Baba looked at me and said: "Yes it will fade, but you will remember a little of this dream whenever you need too." With that, I saw Sai Baba turn into a television camera. "I see everything. You need only ask" When I awoke I was amazed that any dream could be so real. I could recall a great deal of the dream but knew that parts were to be remembered in the future. (Much of it was very personal.) I continued to have many vivid dreams about Sai Baba and so did my wife Jane. They were so compelling, so real, and so mysterious that they were to lead us on a wonderful spiritual adventure to India. When we got to Sai Baba's ashram in India, we met many other people who were called via lucid dream, including some who claimed Sai Baba appeared before them in his physical form. Some seekers have been fortunate enough to talk about their dreams with Sai Baba, who was able to tell them every detail of their dream and the exact words they dreamed he'd said to them.

In his book, *My Baba and I*, Dr John Hislop gives a fascinating example of this ability to bi-locate. Victoria, Hislop's wife, began to ask Sai Baba about an experience she'd had when she was one year old, when her mother was teaching her to walk. In the corner of the room, she remembered seeing a man and she called out to him, "Dada," and took a few steps forward. However, this puzzled her for she had just left her father in the room:

At this point in the story, Baba interrupted and said, "Yes, yes, I was there. I was standing against the wall like this." Swamiji then stretched out his legs, crossing one over the other. Then he continued, "I had a cloth around my head like this." He illustrated by moving his hand around his head, "And I had a cloth around my waist." And, indeed that was what Victoria had seen.

The spiritually advanced teachers from India remind us that both the waking and dreaming states exist in the mind. Even what we call reality is in fact an illusion, a dream from which we will one day awaken. Men and women who have seen through the illusion realize that reality is a dream. Or as they say in Tibet: "As images seen in a dream, thus should one see all things."

The adept who has truly awakened gains mastery not only over dreams but also over matter itself. Enlightened beings have the power to materialize items at will or to be in many places at the same time. The student who succeeds in understanding that his life is a dream that he himself supplies with pleasant or terrifying scenes can ensure that the dream does not become a nightmare. By controlling your dreams you begin to control your destiny.

According to many Eastern teachings, many yogis use lucid dreams to attain higher consciousness. Tibetan Buddhism tells that adepts of the meditative arts retain consciousness throughout dreaming and dreamless sleep. In other words, all their dreams are lucid. Tibetan teachings also advise the dreamer that, although lucid dreams can be very pleasurable, ultimately the dreamer must go beyond the phantasmagoria they watch and play a part in. This only increases the desire to remain spiritually asleep. Enlightenment--awakening--is the goal.

Today many scientists are studying lucid dreams and believe that they can be therapeutic. The ability to control the events in dreams increases the dreamer's ability to take control of his own life and face up to difficulties and challenges. Using these dreams the dreamer can reach into the unconscious, have deeper levels of self-knowledge, and unlock creative potential.

For those who have acquired the knack of lucidity, the benefits can be enormous: Lucid dreaming gives you the chance to experience amazing inner adventures rarely surpassed elsewhere in life. These experiences can increase creativity and promote personal growth and self-confidence. In addition, scientific studies have shown that there is a strong connection between dreams and the biological functioning of the body. Lucid dreaming may be able to improve both your mental and physical health. In short, lucid dreaming is good for you.

Scientists have now developed lucid dream techniques aimed at help ordinary dreamers "turn" lucid:

LUCID DREAM EXPERIMENT 1
TRIGGERING AND RECALLING LUCID DREAMS

There are now many techniques available to help you trigger and recall lucid dreams but the simplest, and in my opinion the most effective, is to ask yourself many times during the day whether you are dreaming.

Objective: To trigger a lucid dream

Step 1: Stop yourself during your daily tasks and ask yourself "Am I dreaming?" Of course, you are not dreaming but each time you ask this question, look for evidence proving you are not dreaming. For example, the most reliable test is to read something, look away for a moment, and then read it again. If what you read is the same twice then it is unlikely that you are dreaming. (By doing this, you are helping to establish a habit of questioning reality and will continue this habit when asleep.)

Step 2: Once you have proved to yourself that you are not presently dreaming, imagine yourself doing something you really love doing. (This time you are associating a controlled fantasy with the act of noticing that you are lucid.) Now tell yourself, "In the same way I will remember and control my dreams." If the situation permits, say this aloud. It will reinforce the habit of questioning reality and of taking control.

Step 3: Continue to practice this technique as many times as you can over the coming weeks. You are trying to remember to wake up in your dream. It's a bit like picking up milk on the way home after reminding yourself to do so an hour before.

Step 4: Before you fall asleep say to yourself, "Tonight I will wake up in my dream." Again, you are reinforcing your inner programming to encourage a lucid dream. At first, triggering a lucid dream takes a lot of effort but it gets easier once lucid dream habits are established.

Step 5: Most people have their first lucid dream when they experience unusual or bizarre occurrences in their dream. You may dream of doing something that is normally impossible such as flying, levitating, or breathing under water. In these dreams, you wake up in the dream as it is taking place. You recognize that what's happening to you is impossible and thereby realize that you are dreaming.

Step 6: Your initial reaction to "waking-up" in a dream is likely to be to actually wake up and you may not be able to retain your lucid dream state for very long. If you do, it is helpful to return to the dream immediately. In this instance, you can break your usual rule of always logging your dreams in your dream diary immediately on awakening. Go back to "sleep" but try to continue with the same dream.

Step 7: As you return to the dream, you will discover that you have some control over the way it progresses. Try gently to steer its course. You may want to change it slightly by adding another character or event that wasn't in the first dream. By doing this you gradually learn to influence and change dreams. Also, remind yourself: "I am dreaming, I want to remember to recognize that I am dreaming." At first, it may be difficult to retain your lucidity for very long and you will fall back into ordinary dreaming. With practice, you will extend your period of control.

Step 8: In the morning, enter the lucid dream into your dream diary. (Write "Lucid Dream" beside it so you can compare it with other lucid dreams you will have in the future.) What was the dream content that first helped it turn lucid? Perhaps next time you dream about this same thing it will again trigger lucid dreaming.

Step 9: Once you've ingrained the question "Is this a dream?" into your consciousness, you can expand the range of questions. You could ask, "How do I know that I am not dreaming?" or "What would be different about this situation if I were dreaming right now?" Again you will need to continually repeat these questions to yourself until you spontaneously ask them in your sleep.

Once you have mastered lucid dreaming, your dreams will never be the same again. The problem of recall will become less because your dreams will be so vivid that it will be hard not to remember them. Your dreams can become almost as clear as normal waking consciousness.

However, not every night should be spent in dream aerobics. Too much of a good thing may interfere with your sleep patterns. I've certainly found in own experience that a series of nights spent lucid dreaming can leave me tired and moody. It is of course exciting to start having lucid dreams, and the temptation is to keep on trying for better and better results. Understand that lucid dreams are most readily achieved with an attitude that is concentrated, persistent, and at the same time playful. You should consider it an enjoyable, creative experience. It is not an act of will but a gentle art.

Reality Testing Methods

During lucid dreams you will become completely aware that you are dreaming as the dream is talking place. However, it is still easy to forget that you are dreaming and slip back into an ordinary dream. The following simple methods will help you attain and maintain consciousness during your lucid dream. All the methods are designed to encourage you to question the reality of your dream and help you realize that you are dreaming. There are many methods you can try and you may enjoy making up your own. Here are some of the most widely used lucid dream techniques:

Look at your hands- Most people find this the simplest way to take control of a dream. By looking for your hands in a dream you use the power of your will to control the dream. This technique was suggested in the books of Carlos Castenada in which he allegedly meets a Yaqi Indian sorcerer who instructs him in the art of dreaming. His teacher Don Juan

Matus tells him to look for his hands while dreaming. This establishes a link between the waking lives and the dreaming lives. Looking at the hands is a cue to lucidity. (In fact any object could act as your lucid dream trigger. For example, you could decide that every time you see a tree in your dream it will act as your inner prompt that you're about to go lucid.)

Dream jumping and flying – Only in dreams can you fly or make superhuman jumps into the air. When you start to become conscious during a dream try this simple reality test: jump into the air and try to prolong your stay up in the air. Even if you stay up for a split second longer than you would in waking life it will prove to you that this is not waking reality. You are dreaming. You can try doing other impossible things such as walking through walls or growing wings. All these illogical events will reinforce the realization that you are dreaming.

Dream Illiteracy – In an ordinary dream it is often difficult to read. Words often appear nonsensical. If you find yourself reading in a dream, prove to yourself that you are dreaming by reading the same thing again. It is most likely that the information you already read will have changed.

Dream memory – When you are awake it is easy to remember what you have been doing over the last few hours. Try doing this in a dream. You will discover that you either have no past at all or a very strange one. This method will help you recognize that you are dreaming, as this is clearly not normal reality.

Change reality – In normal waking life only people like Uri Geller can influence the material world with the power of the mind. However in a dream anything is possible. Pick up an object from your dream and see if you can bend it with the power of your mind. If the object bends to your mental command you are obviously dreaming.

IMPROVING LUCID RECALL

According to many Eastern religions, all life is a dream. To start remembering to awaken from a dream is to begin lifting the veil of illusion. The Hindus call this "Maya." Maya is the dream we dream while awake, the illusion that this is all there is. Realizing the illusory nature of dreams you have in sleep may help you see through the illusion of what you believe to be reality. Lucid dreams may be a useful tool to help you attain spiritual realization and enlightenment.

In dreaming, the brain relies on its own internal stimulation rather than external stimulation to create the dream situations, characters, and dreamscapes. It is a complete inner world but is as much part of reality as is perception of the outer world. Both worlds are constructed by the workings of the brain. This book that you now hold in your hands and read is actually a picture, with sensations of touch, that is formed in your head by information given to the brain by your perceptions. It is a picture reconstructed by the chemistry and electrical conditions of your brain.

You cannot prove what reality is. Many mystics believe that realities exist outside normal awareness but that can be accessed through dreams. Once you master lucid dreaming, anything is possible.

By following the exercises and techniques in this book you are probably now able to recall more than one dream per night. You have developed a rapport with your unconscious, realize that dreams are important and useful, and are more likely to be able to move into the lucid dream state. Increasing your ability to recall was your first and most difficult step. And most importantly, you have created within yourself the desire to master the art of dreaming. Without intent, dream recall is difficult. Just as the desire to have a dream increased the likelihood that you would have one, so too your desire to have a lucid dream will increase the likelihood you will also have one.

Lucid dreaming is a form of dream recall in which you remember the dream as it is taking place. Lucid dreams are easier to remember than ordinary dreams but you should continue to note them in your dream diary and continue to use the recall methods that you mastered earlier in this book.

Using REM Cycles to Improve Lucid Dreaming.

One of the first ways suggested to remember a dream is to set the alarm to ring earlier than usual to interrupt a REM period (when your eyes rapidly move beneath the lids as you dream). There are products on the market that can detect eye movement and turn a light on, causing you to become aware that you are dreaming without waking up. These are very good products. It is also possible to interrupt a REM cycle without having to wear this special sleep mask.

Objective: The object of the next experiment is to wake up before you have finished sleeping and then return from an ordinary dream state to a lucid dream state. Try this over the weekend when you have no work obligations.

Step 1: Sleep cycles last from about 90 to 120 minutes. Set your alarm to go off 100 minutes before you ordinarily wake up so you interrupt the start of your next dream cycle.

Step 2: When the alarm wakes you, remain awake for the whole cycle before returning to sleep (100 minutes).

Step: 3 When the time has elapsed go back to sleep.

Step 4: Within about five minutes you will begin to have vivid dreams. By waking up early, and staying awake for a full REM cycle you have deprived yourself of essential dream time. You have created a temporary REM deficit, which leads into extended REM once you return to sleep. Your dreams are likely to quickly become very intense.

Step 5: Use this opportunity of intense dreaming to seize control of the dream.

GETTING UP TOO EARLY

A REM deficit occurs if you get up too early. When you are deprived of this essential period of dreaming, your mind will compensate at the earliest opportunity. If you take a catnap in the afternoon, you are likely to immediately go straight into a dream cycle because of the REM deficit from the morning. You will increase the likelihood of turning these dreams into lucid dreams if you can hold yourself on the brink between waking and sleeping.

Some of the most vivid dreams of my life occurred when I worked on a kibbutz in Israel. We would get up at 3.00 a.m. and work in the fields until 11.00 a.m. After breakfast we would take a siesta. These catnaps were extraordinary experiences as I was thrown into an immediate lucid dream state. In one of these "dreams" I saw the city of Haifa being destroyed by an earthquake. At the next day's work session in the banana groves I started to tell a friend about my vivid dream. Within seconds, the ground beneath us started to shake.

It was only a minor earth tremor and not the cataclysmic disaster I saw in my lucid dream but the experience demonstrated to me in a startling way that lucid dreams can give us access to information through clairvoyance.

TIBETAN LUCID DREAM CONTROL

Once you have mastered becoming conscious while a dream is taking place, the next step is to take control of the dream. This all sounds very dramatic but is a very old art and is accessible to anyone who is prepared to work with dreams. Dream control is an integral part of the mystical teachings of Tibetan yoga and of many shamanic traditions. Tibetan

Buddhists believe that controlling dreams gives control in the realms after death.

One of the most important Tibetan Buddhist texts is the *Bardo Thodol*, better known as *The Tibetan Book of the Dead*, which explains how to travel in the worlds beyond death and also gives guidance about controlling the dream-state. Bardo means "intermediate state" and denotes the period that lies between a person's death and his rebirth. *Thodol*, pronounced *Thos Grol*, means "liberation through understanding." The *Bardo Thodol* is a "treasure text," which means it is attributed to Shakyamuni Buddha himself.

According to the *Bardo Thodol*, we can divide our existence into four interlinked realities: life, dying and death, after death, and rebirth. These are called the four *bardos*: the natural *bardo* of this earthly life, the painful *bardo* of dying, the luminous *bardo* of *dharmata* and the karmic *bardo* of becoming. (*Bardo* is a Tibetan word that translates as "transition." *Bar* means "in between" and *do* means "suspended.") These texts are read to the dying and are believed to help them either enter the light of pure consciousness or attain a better rebirth. Many lamas occupy themselves with the writings of the *Bardo Thodol* throughout their lives and not just at the time of death.

Bardos have been likened to a gap, or a period in which the possibility of awakening to higher consciousness is present. These opportunities can happen at times of great uncertainty, particularly when dying, but also, to a lesser extent, at times of crisis. To the Tibetan Buddhist, the turbulent uncertainty that prevails modern life provides plenty of opportunity to experience the *bardos* without having to die to do it!

Bardos are opportunities but at the same time they are the inner incentive that drives you to seize the opportunity they offer. They can represent different states of reality as well as different states of consciousness. Tibetan Buddhists believe that lucid dreams are a doorway into these sought-after states of consciousness.

TIBETAN CLOUD WALKING

According to the Tibetans, going to sleep is similar to the *bardo* of dying. In deep sleep the elements and thought processes dissolve and open into the experience of the "Ground Luminosity" (described as the dawning nature of the mind). Also, there is a *bardo* to be found between the period after falling asleep and before dreams begin. This is called the *bardo dharmata* and is said to be the "radiance of the nature of the mind," also known as the "Clear Light."

Dreaming is akin to the karmic *bardo* of becoming, which to the dying person is the intermediate state that lasts right up to the moment of taking a new birth. In this state the dreamer has a clairvoyant and highly mobile "dream body" (also translated as the "mental body").

The "dream body" is similar to the duplicate etheric body described by mediums and by Spiritualists called the "spirit body." Similarly, the Hindus describe it as the "subtle body," which carries the *Jiva*, personal self, into the afterlife or to the next incarnation. It is a body made of life energy and appears as light. It is a spiritual duplicate of the physical body.

While in the dream body you feel extremely light, lucid, and mobile. The Tibetans tell us that its awareness is seven times clearer than in life. In this form you are endowed with clairvoyance and, in particular, have the power of telepathy, the ability to read minds or communicate by thought. The "dream body" can pass through walls and go wherever it wishes unobstructed. If you think of place or person, you are instantly transported there by the power of thought. In this *bardo* world, you can meet many other travelers and converse with the spirits of people who have died.

The *Tibetan Book of the Dead* says that it is very difficult to retain awareness while in the "dream body" while still alive. The experience of these states at death is of course far more powerful than anything experienced in sleep. The Tibetan masters also teach that remaining conscious during the dream state can prepare a person for death because, as in ordinary dreams, the spirit can lose awareness the after death state. Also, say the Tibetans, the state of your mind in the sleep state and dream states indicates how your mind will be in the corresponding *bardo*-states after death. According to the Tibetans, the way you react to dreams and nightmares shows how you might react when you die.

Tibetans therefore consider lucid dreaming to be a high form of spiritual yoga and as important as meditation. Meditation is the yoga of the day and lucid dreaming is the yoga of the night.

LEARNING TO FLY

Many lucid dreamers claim they dream of being able to fly. It is a thrilling means of travel. Many dream flyers claim it is a real experience that transcends the illusory dream state. Some find deliberate dream flying a useful tool that has helped them return from the nightmare of an endless fall. Dream flying usually brings with it a feeling of safety, exhilaration, and pleasure.

Objective: In this first flying lesson, you will fly using lucid dreaming techniques. By practicing these methods, you will gain greater mastery over dreams. It is one more step toward complete recall, as you retain your waking consciousness during sleep.

Dreaming of flying is a form of dream control that is easy to master. It is great fun, gives you a wonderful sense of freedom, and is the perfect means of travel in the dream world.

Step 1: Whatever you focus your attention on grows in strength. Over the next few weeks pay particular attention to dreams that hint at dream flight. Note any symbols of flight, such as dreams about birds, airplanes, and so on. You may spontaneously dream about flying or falling. Many people dream of falling as they "fall" to sleep. This can be caused by a drop in blood pressure or the movement of the fluid in the middle ear. Turn your fall into a flight.

Step 2: Whenever you become aware that you are dreaming try to turn all movements into flight. Fly rather than walk. You can reinforce this during your waking life by imagining what it would be like if you could fly to your destination. Every time you take a stroll, think about flying. This will help you to condition yourself to fly in dreams.

Step 3: Before you go to sleep use dream incubation to encourage a dream about flying. In bed repeat these words: "tonight I fly." As you say them, imagine yourself flying. Think about all the different landscapes you could fly over and remember the times you have flown in an airplane.

Step 4: If you find yourself flying, you are of course dreaming. Once you realize that you are dreaming you will be reminded of your desire to fly. As you continue flying say to yourself: "This is a dream." This will increase your lucidity and help you remain conscious throughout the dream.

Step 5: As you become comfortable with this unusual state, you may want to try a few experiments. You can try jumping off cliffs, leaping high into the air, or running at high speed, taking huge steps before you take off. Win your cosmic pilot's wings by the continual practice of your flying skills. Of course you cannot hurt yourself, but take it easy at first just in case so you don't get scared.

Step 6: If you become skilled at "waking up" during flying dreams you may want to try experiments to test the limits of this state. For example, can you fly to the moon or Mars? How high can you fly? Can you fly through brick walls? How fast can you go? This dream fantasy will bring you hours of fun!

LINDBERGH'S ASTRAL FLIGHT

Charles Lindbergh was the U.S. aviator who made the first solo nonstop flight across the Atlantic Ocean from New York to Paris in 1927. In the 22nd hour into his flight aboard his monoplane Spirit of St Louis he was enveloped in a dense fog. He battled to keep in control, on course, and awake.

Fifty years later he recalled: "I existed independently of time and matter. I felt myself departing from my body as I imagine a spirit would depart--emanating into the cockpit, extending through the fuselage as though no frame of fabric walls were there, angling upward, outward, until I reformed in an awareness far distant from the human form I left in a fast-flying transatlantic plane. But I remained connected to my body through a long-extended strand, a strand so tenuous that it could have been severed by a breath."

He denied that his experience was a hallucination brought on by extreme fatigue. In his autobiography he wrote: "My visions are easily explained away through reason, but the longer I live, the more limited I believe rationality to be."

OUT-OF-BODY DREAMS

In the last experiment, your flying dream was fantasy. It is a useful method to help you recall dreams by intensifying your lucidity. But what if it were actually possible to fly? Supposing there was a way to have a real flying experience. Supposing you could step out of your physical body and fly over the Earth and through strange new worlds.

Many philosophies and religions believe that the spirit and the body exist separately and that the spirit body survives after death. Many people also believe that it is possible for the spiritual body to journey outside the physical body during deep meditation, at a time of extreme shock, critical illness, or during dreams.

In this next experiment, you will learn to leave your physical body. Once you perfect this technique you will be able to access the planes of existence that contain the collective storehouse of human knowledge and memory that mystics call the "akashic record."

EXPERIMENT:
HOW TO TRAVEL IN THE DREAM BODY

Dr Eugene E. Barnard has estimated that one out of every 100 people experiences out-of-body travel at some time during their lifetime. It is certainly not a new phenomenon and descriptions can be found in many ancient texts. For example, the ancient Egyptians thought of the astral body, or ba, as a birdlike spirit with a human head. In the Old Testament, the prophet Elisha is described as moving through the air into the bedroom of the hostile Syrian king. Here he overheard the king's military plans and was able to warn the Israelites of the forthcoming Syrian attack. Mystics have given this spiritual body many different names including the astral body, the body of light, the duplicate body, the etheric body, and the dream body.

In modern times, Theosophy and Spiritualism took a great interest in OBE phenomena. The British physicist and vocal Spiritualist Sir Oliver Lodge undertook a great deal of research into OBEs. He was also a member of the Society for Psychical Research, which in 1886 published a collaborative work by its leading members called *Phantasms of the Living*. This massive two-volume book by SPR members Edmund Gurney, Frederic Myers, and Frank Podmore took three years to compile and was hugely influential. It cataloged 702 cases of "crisis apparitions," or appearances of the dead at or immediately after the moment of death. It also cited many instances where the apparitions were of living people who had temporarily left their moral frame. Some instances told of cases where people claimed to have purposely willed their discarnate selves to appear in the view of others.

One of the most famous contemporary out-of-body travelers was businessman Robert Monroe. He had his first OBE in 1958 and initially thought he might be hallucinating or going insane. He was at first shocked and distressed at what was happening to him. However, soon he began to enjoy his out-of-body journeys and delighted in his amazing discoveries.

Monroe began to log his explorations into the non-corporal worlds in a dream journal. He kept meticulous records and participated in laboratory experiments to find out more about the phenomenon. In 1971, he published *Journeys Out of the Body*. This first-person account of his multi-dimensional journeys became a bestseller. Eventually Monroe gave up his business and concentrated full time on his OBE experiments. Today The Monroe Institute is dedicated to the research and understanding of OBE phenomena.

This next experiment is based loosely on Monroe's recommendations:

Objective: To travel in the dream body.

Step 1: Lie on your bed in a dark room and in a comfortable position. If possible, lie with your head pointing north. The Earth's magnetic field will help your release. (Some modern mystics think that the special alignments of places such as Stonehenge and the Pyramids were designed to enable the ancient people to have OBEs. In one OBE of my own, these places had an irresistible pull. My own feeling is that they are signposts to the astral realm. They point the way or act as reference points by using the powers of the Earth's energies. You become conscious of these energies when moving in the astral body.)

Step 2: Let yourself relax completely. Close your eyes and become aware how your breathing slows. It becomes more rhythmical as you sink deeper into total relaxation. You may want to reread the relaxation experiments in the first part of this book in order to ensure that you relax as completely as possible. This is a very important.

Step 3: As you drift toward sleep focus on a single image. Once you are in a state that is neither sleep nor wakefulness deepen your relaxation by concentrating on the blackness beyond your eyelids.

Step 4: Now focus on a point about 12 inches (30 cm) from your forehead. Gradually extend the point of focus to a distance of about six feet (1.8 m). Some people find it easier to focus on a tangible object such as a light fixture or a mark on the ceiling. Keep your eyes closed but imagine that you are drawing it toward you. When an OBE takes place, you will realize that it is not being drawn toward you. You are being drawn toward it! This is one way also to move around the astral world. Imagine drawing objects toward yourself. This will help you move in the astral form. If you *think* movement, it becomes a fact.

Step 5: Imagine that there is a line parallel to your body. Focus on this plane and imagine that vibrations are running down it and toward you and into your head. Monroe claims that awareness of vibrations is a sign that you are close to an OBE. In my own experiments I usually become aware of a deep purple light at this stage and am aware that I can see the room even though my eyes are closed.

Step 6: Once this feeling of vibration becomes clear then you are ready to leave your body. You may find it easier to imagine the vibration as a pulsing light that fills you. Alternatively, perhaps you are better working with sound vibrations. For example, inwardly chanting the Hindu "om" mantra can increase you awareness. Use the imagination to trigger the sensations that accompany an OBE.

Step 7: To leave the body concentrate on how pleasant it would be to float upward. You may imagine that the physical body is heavy like clay whereas you are as light as a feather. You are a wisp of fine smoke. You may prefer a more dynamic image. You can imagine that you are in an elevator or aboard a rocket. If sound appeals to you, you may imagine that the mantra is rising in pitch. You could think words such as "up," "flying," "lightness," "feathers," "clouds," and so on. You may be aware of physical sensations as you leave your body. For example, you may alternate your awareness between the heavy sensation of the physical body and the lightness of your spirit.

Step 8: These techniques will become easier with practice. Try them every time you go to bed. Eventually you will have the sensation of floating upward and leaving your physical body.

Step 9: To return to the physical body is much easier and there is no danger that you will be "locked out." Simply think about the physical body and the two entities will re-engage.

When I was a teenager, I had my first out-of-body experience. I was so shocked to see my body lying on the bed, I panicked. The result was that I re-entered my body like a whiplash. I heard a loud bang like a gun firing, and there was a brilliant flash of white light. I awakened drenched in sweat.

This need not happen to you. At the time, I had never heard about astral traveling so my immediate assumption was that I was dead. The shock triggered a very fast return to the physical body, which resulted in the uncomfortable sensations I experienced. Remain calm and your OBEs will be pleasant experiences.

DREAM BODY SENSATIONS AND PERCEPTIONS

- PARALYSIS: As you come close to an OBE, you will have the feeling that the body is rigid. You may feel that you cannot manipulate your own limbs.
- WEIGHTLESSNESS: When you separate from the physical body, you will experience a feeling of weightlessness. This can be a very enjoyable feeling that brings with it a feeling of freedom.
- ATTACHMENT: Some claim to see a silver umbilical cord that joins the astral and physical bodies. It attaches from the astral body to the head of the physical body. As the two bodies move farther apart the cord becomes thinner but will not break.
- PERCEPTIONS: You will experience colors as being preternaturally sharp and vivid. You will have a heightened awareness of sound.
- VITALITY: The physical body will appear dull and lifeless whereas your astral self will feel vital, energetic, and alive.
- MOVEMENT: Think of a place and you will go there immediately. You can slow down or increase your movements by focusing on the physical objects around you. Draw then to you very slowly and you will add grace to your astral movements.

THIRD EYE

Out of body travel can be further improved if you learn to open your spiritual center called the "Third Eye." This is one of the vital chakras, which are wheels of spiritual energy found at various focal points on the body.

The first chakra is found at the base of the spine at the coccyx, the second is just below the navel, the third is at the solar plexus just below the rib cage, the fourth approximates to the level of the heart, the fifth comes at the level of the throat, and the sixth is at the eyebrow level. This sixth chakra is nicknamed the "third eye" and above it, at the top of the head is the seventh chakra, called the crown chakra. As the spiritual energies rise through these centers the person becomes more spiritually aware and can develop psychic and paranormal powers.

For centuries, the sixth chakra at the third eye has been considered the point where the spirit and body meet. As long ago as the fourth century B.C., Herophilus described it as the organ that regulated the flow of thought. (He compared it to the sphincter!) Its position at the center of the forehead and just above the eyebrows is directly horizontal to the pineal gland, which is located in the center of the brain. This tiny but important gland controls the production of hormones that influence consciousness. When you meditate or concentrate on the center of the forehead you influence this gland. Melatonin is manufactured by the pineal gland through the action of a hormone upon serotonin, a chemical messenger that transmits nerve impulses across synapses. It is thought that these chemicals are somehow connected to the higher functions in people. This appears to confirm the mystical significance of this area of the brain.

During out-of-body travel, a silver cord emanating from near the third eye links the spiritual self to the body.

Earlier you learnt how to open the throat chakra in order to stimulate dream activity. In the next experiment you will open this center again and also the third eye center. This technique can be used before the out-of-body experiment explained earlier and will make it easier to stimulate out-of-body travel. In addition, it is likely to increase the lucidity of your normal dreams should you fall asleep during the experiment.

The objective of these out of body experiments is to access information that is normally denied you. They increases your ability to recall ordinary dreams but also gives you admission to the "akashic record," the cosmic register of all phenomena throughout history.

THIRD EYE CHAKRA EXPERIMENT:

Objective: To open the chakras in order to travel in the dream body and increase the vividness of your dreams.

Step 1: Lying flat on your back, allow yourself to relax very deeply.

Step 2: Visualize a brilliant blue light unfolding at the top of the throat chakra. See it open like a lotus flower of brilliant blue light. You may feel a slight sensation in your throat as this center opens and you may feel your head push backward into your pillow.

Step 3: Now see the light gradually move upward toward the center of the forehead. As it does, the color turns a beautiful purple. This is the color associated with the third eye, but you may also see many other splendid colors as this center unfolds.

Step 4: As this lotus unfolds, be aware of how the purple light now floods the whole head. Bathe yourself in this beautiful soothing radiance. Notice that you also feel a slight tightening around your whole head as this center gradually opens. You may notice many beautiful multi-colored lights coming from your peripheral vision.

Step 5: Once this center is activated, you can continue with the out-of-body experiment you tried in the previous experiment. You will have at your disposal great quantities of psychic energy when you open this center in this way.

Step 6: Only try this experiment occasionally as it uses a great amount of spiritual energy if you go to sleep with your third eye center open. You may feel extremely sensitive in the morning.

Step 7: After any experiments with the chakras, is important to close them down. If you awaken after an OBE, or first thing in the morning, you should close the center as soon as you are ready. To do this, imagine that the energy in the center is quieting down. Then see it gradually fade to darkness as the lotus flower closes its petals. All is still. Light can get neither in or out. It is closed.

Result: Doing this technique as you fall to sleep will increase the vividness of your dreams and improve your ability to project the dream body.

SHARED DREAM MEMORIES

Out-of-body travelers claim that they meet people from other regions of existence. This may include other dimensions, the afterlife spheres, the angelic kingdoms, the elemental regions of nature, and even the astral worlds of other planets. Some of this may be real but much may be fantasy. To prove to yourself that your OBE experiences are real, do this next dream experiment with a friend or with a group of spiritually minded friends. It will sharpen your recall ability because you and your team are going to remember the same dream!

I WILL MEET YOU IN MY DREAMS

Objective: To meet your friend/s in a dream. A "communicator" will bring with them a target image that is to be "seen" by the other dreamers (the receivers).

Step 1: Chose one of your team to be the dream "communicator" for the night's experiment. It is best if this person is a good lucid dreamer or has had previous out-of-body dreams. The rest of the team will be dream receivers.

Step 2: Plan to meet in your dreams at a landmark known by all of you. Chose somewhere that is easily recognized yet not too busy at night. For example, you could arrange to meet in the city art gallery beside a specific painting or sculpture, at a statue in the park, or on top of a tall public building. Distance makes no difference but it needs to be a place that is known well by all of you.

Step 3: You will now all agree to meet in your dreams at this place on a specific night. When you get there, you will all look for the communicator who will show the rest of the team an image only known to him/her. If you have a number of people working together, you can have two or more communicators who will decide secretly in advance, what the target image will be. This will increase the likelihood of someone being at the site to transmit the target image when the receivers arrive.

Step 4: The communicator/s should decide the target image and go to bed knowing what it is. For example, if the chosen image is a box of corn flakes, the communicator should put a box of corn flakes beside the bed. This will reinforce the picture in the communicator's mind. You can choose anything you like that would be feasible to carry in real life: a cuddly toy, a newspaper, a cup of tea, a funny hat, a mask, and so on.

Step 5: Do the lucid dream or dream body experiments and attempt to move toward the target venue. You have only to think about the location and you will go to it. Team members should put a photograph of the place beside their bed to reinforce the image. (If you choose a well-known landmark, you could use a postcard.)

Step 6: Communicators should attempt to show the selected object to the dreamers they meet at the landmark. If they see members of the team they should give them the object or make them aware of what it is. For example, if the target object is a box of corn flakes, the communicator should shake it so they hear it. Also, feed them some so they taste it. Hold the box in front of them and even make then touch it. Get all the senses involved so the image is shown in as many different ways as possible. If you get to the target landmark and nobody is there, leave the imaginary box of corn flakes at the location. If you are a receiver and you get to the deserted landmark, look around to see if you can see any unusual objects.

Step 7: Some of you will have very strong lucid dreams about the location. However, do not dismiss dreams that are not about the target place. The information you are looking for may be hidden in what appears to be an ordinary dream.

Step 8: When you wake up, note in your dream diary what you saw. No matter how insignificant it is, write it down. Note everything you dreamed that night, even if there appears to be no hint of the target location.

Step 9: Once you have recorded your notes, you and your friends should get together as soon as possible. Go through your dream diary entries and see if your dreams have any similarities. You are likely to discover that the dream target has been changed in some way. For example, if you were shown the box of corn flakes you may have dreamed of eating or perhaps you dreamed that you were grocery shopping in a supermarket. You may not have seen the target image exactly but you nonetheless understood the nature of the image that was being given to you.

You may also find that many of your dreams have similar themes that have nothing to do with the target location or image. This may indicate that you and your team are developing a telepathic rapport. You are communicating thoughts but not yet traveling out of the body. When your conscious mind relaxes in sleep, your psychic abilities are at their peak And in dreams you can communicate our inner thoughts to people we know.

6 REMEMBERING PAST LIVES

The soul in sleep gives proof of its divine nature.
Marcus Tullius Cicero (106-43 BC)
Roman orator and statesman

Have you ever thought that you may have lived before? A growing number of people now believe in reincarnation, the philosophy that says that after death the soul transmigrates and is born again in a new body. Many people today also believe in metempsychosis, which proposes that you can also be born into an animal form after death or that you may have been an animal before becoming a human. For example, if a person lives like a pig or a snake in this life the person may be reincarnated as a snake or a pig.

Belief in reincarnation has been with us a long time. The Vedas--the 9,000-year-old texts of the Hindus--teach that the soul (Jiva) moves from body to body over eons of time. It may sojourn for a while in the heavenly worlds, if it has done good deeds while on earth, but it will in time reincarnate again in order to evolve spiritually. Its ultimate goal is to realize its unity with God. Many other Eastern religions believe in reincarnation. Tibetan Buddhists believe that highly evolved souls, such as the Dalai Lama, can choose which womb they will be born from for their next life. On the death of a great lama a search is organized to discover the whereabouts of the new baby Lama. Occasionally these souls are born to Western families.

But the belief in reincarnation is not limited to the East. Orpheus, Pythagoras, Plato, and certain Gnostics and Kabbalists explicitly referred to reincarnation in their writings. Some historians believe that the early Christians may have held similar beliefs. For example, many believers in reincarnation say that the migrating soul accumulates karma. This is the potential carried by a person that dictates what good and bad things will befall the person. It is determined by the good and bad actions in this life. Similarly, the fruits of an earlier life are carried on to the next. Some argue that when Jesus said, "As you sow so shall you reap," he was referring to the cosmic laws of karma and reincarnation.

Today many spiritual and psychological techniques have been devised in order to access our lost memories of earlier existences. Regressive hypnosis, meditation, visualization exercises, aura awareness, channeling, and so on are all effective. But perhaps the simplest and safest method is the spontaneous insight that can come through dream recall.

DREAMING TO REMEMBER CHILDHOOD

One of the most mysterious qualities about dreams is their ability to recall events as if they happened only moments ago. Most of us have had dreams about our childhood. The settings, the people and the atmosphere can be tremendously vivid. Yet if we try to recall these things in waking life they are just fuzzy and half-remembered events. We all have a number of childhood memories that are clear in our minds, but in dreams old memories come alive. In a dream we may meet our childhood friends and enemies and it feels as if a single day hasn't passed. Dreams open parts of the memory that are normally inaccessible.

In order to recall past lives you must first train the subconscious to recall as much of your childhood as it can. Initially you may be content with the pleasure at remembering childhood memories but later you can push your dreams back to the time of your birth and then back even further to your past lives.

Of course you must also proceed with care. Not all childhood memories are good ones, and you may uncover the source of many of your inner fears. Proceed gently, one step at a time, and be prepared to discover both good and bad things about yourself. Approach this hidden world with a spirit of acceptance, and be honest with yourself in recognizing your strengths and weaknesses.

The thoughts and feelings you have before going to sleep can easily determine your dreams. Just as your dreams can be influenced by a television program you watched before going to bed, so too your dreams can be influenced by suggestions just before going to sleep. Before going to sleep say to yourself: "Tonight I will dream about my childhood". Say it aloud many times, as this will strengthen the suggestion. You can also reinforce the inner commands by looking at photographs of your childhood or photos of places that remind you of your childhood.

By using these techniques regularly every night you will soon start dreaming about your childhood. Influencing dreams this way is called dream incubation. The brain is like a biological computer that can be programmed. Asking your unconscious to do specific things while you sleep helps you control your feelings and worries. These techniques give you a command over the subconscious and can increase your self-confidence.

Write down any dreams that come to you and pay particular attention to dreams that remind you of your childhood. You may want to spend some time thinking about associated memories. For example, if you dream about being at school, spend some time remembering everything you can about the place. Think about your old friends, the teachers, the smells, the sounds, the times you did well, and the times you got in trouble. Take an imaginary journey down its corridors. Relive your time there as if it were only yesterday. Your dreams will help you bring the past alive and your memories will become astonishingly vivid.

The past lives of George S. Patton (1885-1945)

George S. Patton was the American general who led the U.S. troops to breach the defenses at Normandy and led a spectacular advance to the Moselle. In the Ardennes he cleared the west bank of the Rhine, crossed it, and encircled the Ruhr. Yet, this great American general believed that he had done his military training in previous lives.

In December 1917, when he visited Langres tank school in northeast France, a local liaison officer showed him around the town. He started to tell Patton about how the area had once been the site of a Roman military camp but was interrupted: "You don't have to," said Patton "I know this place. I know it well" he then directed the driver around the ruins and could point out the various landmarks. He knew the drill ground, the temples of Mars and Apollo, the forum and the amphitheater, yet he had never been to the town before in his life.

Patton believed that he had been to France before as a Roman legionnaire. He even knew the exact spot where Julius Caesar had made his camp. "It was as if someone were at my ear whispering the direction." He later told his nephew.

Patton was forthright in his conviction that his military successes were a continuation of campaigns he had waged in previous lives. He had memories of being at the walls of Tyre with Alexander the Great and of being a member of the Greek phalanx which met Cyrus II, the Persian warlord who established the Achaemenid empire in 500 B.C. He also believed he fought at Crécy's Field during the Hundred Years War.

During the North African campaign of World War Two, a British soldier quipped "You would have made a great marshal for Napoleon if you'd lived in the 18th century." Patton looked back at the soldier. A wry grin broke across his face. "But I did," he replied.

DREAMING TO REMEMBER YOUR BIRTH

Once you've established a pattern of remembering early childhood memories the next step is to encourage your subconscious to recall your very first memories from when you were a baby and right back to the moment you were born. Look through your dream diary to see if any of your dreams relate to early childhood. You may be surprised how many there are. Dreams take no notice of time. In dreams, memories from your early years are just as vivid as the ones you can recall from yesterday.

It is a fascinating exercise to see just how much you can remember from your early life. For example, I have a hazy memory of being in the pram. I am aware of the sunshine streaming into my warm resting-place. I feel wonderfully comfortable and at ease with the world and myself. Lined across the hood of the pram I can see red and yellow shapes that make a rattle sound when I hit them. I can remember my frustration at not quite being able to hit them with my tiny hands. According to my mother, four plastic ducks threaded with elastic were stretched across the hood of my pram. They were yellow and red. Beads would rattle if I hit them.

Practice remembering your childhood. Many of the techniques you have already learned can be applied to remembering long-forgotten people, events, and places from your distant past. Take another look at the section about dream recall and use the techniques to recover ordinary memories as well as dream memories. Can you remember the wallpaper in your bedroom? What was your favorite childhood food? How many Christmas mornings and birthdays can you recall? Can you remember being reprimanded and praised?

We tend to think that we have long forgotten about the events of our own birth, but even if our conscious mind has forgotten, recorded in our unconscious is everything and every event that ever happened to us, including our birth experience. Rebirthing therapists point out that birth is a traumatic experience that is remembered by the body on a cellular level. The baby's experience of the pain of birth, the cutting of the umbilical cord, the drugs used at birth, and clinical procedures result in trauma. Memories of birth are soon repressed but will re-emerge in adulthood as behavioral flaws and social maladjustment. A study done at San. Quentin, a high security prison in California, showed that over 80% of the inmates had had violent births. These included cesareans or births that involved invasive procedures and instruments.

It is claimed that recalling the trauma of birth can help you overcome many unexplained fears and anxieties. For our purpose birth recall is a stepping stone to the time before you were born and the lives you led before your spirit entered your mother's womb.

By working with the childhood memories given to you by your dreams you will also draw closer to the unconscious memories you have of birth and of being in the womb. As you did earlier, you need now to encourage your subconscious to remember this event and reveal it to you in a dream. This time, as you go to sleep say to yourself: "Tonight I will dream about my birth." Say it aloud many times to strengthen the suggestion. You have set your biological computer to run with a new program.

If you dream about your birth, you may experience the sensation of floating in the womb, being attached to the umbilical cord, being pushed down a dark tunnel, or feeling vulnerable. These dreams can be accompanied by many strange sensations that are hard to describe. Because of this, your dreams are likely to translate your birth and womb experiences into symbols such as floating in or swimming under the sea.

Here's an example from my own dream diary that I believe relates to the moment of my birth. It is a dream that has recurred throughout my life, particularly during my childhood.

I feel warm and secure. I have a feeling of floating and of well-being. Now there is a rumbling sound. My skin feels tight, as if my whole body is enfolded in rubber. I feel pressure all over. I have a sense of suffocation. The sounds get louder. The warm feeling of security changes to one of anxiety and resistance. I am aware of a pathway. It is lined on either side by small primrose flowers. I can hear the voices of crowds of people, as if I am in a restaurant or railway station. I am now aware of a thick rope close to my face. Now it becomes thin like fragile cotton. Again it becomes a rope. My fingers feel numb. Once more I am crushed, particularly around my head. I see an extraordinary bright, bright light. I feel fear. I wake up but cannot shake off the horrible feeling of this nightmare.

I'm sure Freud would have had plenty to say about what my dream revealed about my resistance to life and my desire to remain in the safe waters of the womb. However, I believe that this dream is a memory of my actual birth. It was very hard to describe because so many of the sensations cannot be related to anything I know. This is likely to be the same confusion that a baby must feel. I understand the rope and cotton to be the umbilical cord, but have no idea what the primroses are. I'm sure the sensations of sound and the bright lights are memories of the moment I came into the world.

All of us retain the memory of birth somewhere in our brain. Dreams are the key to recalling this most important experience. In my extract I called the dream a nightmare. Clearly birth recall is not always a pleasant experience but I'm sure it is of benefit to remember and integrate the experience. At one time the dream would force itself upon me. It has not reoccurred since I wrote it down.

This dream proved to me that it was possible to remember just about anything in dreams. If I could remember as far back as my birth would it not be possible to remember even further back, to the time before I was born?

By working with your dreams in a systematic way you will gradually move back further in your memories to the time before you were born. You have already established the habit of using dreams as an aid to recalling memories from this life, so it is not a big step to shift your attention to lives before you were born. Of course some of these dreams may be fantasy but others will ring true. Ideally you may receive some information that you can confirm by checking the public records, but in most instances the experience will be subjective.

The Tibetan Buddhist Dzogchen sect believes that it is very beneficial to remember your birth. The most important Tibetan Buddhist text that covers the subject of what lies beyond death and the means to seek a fortuitous new birth is *Bardo Thodol*, better known as *The Tibetan Book of the Dead*. (See page XXX for a discussion of this work.) Bardo means "intermediate state," and denotes the period between the death and rebirth. Thodol, (pronounced "Thos Grol"), means "liberation through understanding."

What I may have experienced in my birth dream was a memory of the Sixth bardo, the state between death and a new birth. This is the "intermediate state," where one searches for a new birth. At the sixth bardo is the choice of merging with the infinite light (I would call this God) or being reincarnated again. Most of us forget this experience. However some great souls retain their knowledge and are born into this life as fully realized and enlightened beings. The rest of us pass across the "river of forgetting" or only half remember the glorious reality of our true nature. Birth memories bring us close to this knowledge of the infinite. It is also the bardo where it is possible to be totally conscious of every life that we have lived and will live in the future.

Whatever you focus your attention on grows in strength. If you spend time thinking about your childhood memories and memories of your birth, your unconscious mind will come to your aid. It is there to help you. Reading this book may also be helping you focus your attention on past-life recall. The more you think about past lives the more likely it is that your dreams will present you with the information you are seeking.

DREAMSCAPES

I have kept dream records since I was a teenager, and some of the recurring dreams appearing in my early dream diaries may relate to past life experiences. For example I have often dreamt about a fishing village in a place that resembles Cornwall, in the southwestern United Kingdom.

Whenever I dream of this place I have an unearthly feeling of deja vu. The dream has occurred so many times, I now know every roll of the hills, every turn in the road, and every field and building. When I awaken from these dreams I always make a note of what I see. I have even drawn a detailed map of the area. As far as I am aware I have never been to this place. One day I may find it. I believe I have a map to prove that I once lived there in a past life.

Dreamscapes have many clues that point to memories of past lives. A dream landscape can take many forms and may have many levels of meaning. Before reading what follows, stop and think about the many landscapes that may have occurred in your dreams. If you have been keeping a dream diary read back over your entries and particularly take notice of settings, terrain, and landscapes. You may want to make a few notes to help jog your memory about the places you have seen in your dreams. Think about the inner landscapes of the mind that are present when you dream. Consider the scenery, the backdrops, the people, and the objects that are part of your dreamscape.

These landscapes can be interpreted in a number of different ways. Most will have nothing to do with past lives but a few may hold important cryptic information that will reveal hidden knowledge.

Childhood Dreamscapes

Many of your dreamscapes will link to memories from childhood. I often have dreams that are set in my childhood home or my grandfather's luscious back garden. Dreams set in childhood settings may be giving us a temporary respite from the troubles of our world. They may remind us who we really are and of our roots. These dreams may reveal deep-seated memories from childhood or be telling you that you've forgotten how to play and should develop a more carefree attitude toward life. Your dreams may also be a symbol for your potential- something that is still at an early stage of development. They could highlight immature attitudes or reveal parts of you that needs reassurance and security.

Your dreams may also be helping you remember past lives, by helping you reach the deep recesses of your memory. Remembering the lost memories from this life is a stepping stone to remembering lost memories from previous lives. There are many examples of children who remember their previous lives. Perhaps these early memories of childhood hold clues to the knowledge of past lives now forgotten.

Symbolic Dreamscapes

Most dreamscapes will be based on your conscious memories. These may represent the way you feel about yourself and your situation. The landscape of your dream is a symbol. For example, suppose you dream of being on vacation at a place you know well. Your dream may be telling you that you need to take a break. Sometimes dreams feature anxieties, such as missing a plane or train. You may dream of carrying too much luggage. In this case your dreamscape represents the need to take it easy. It is the place where everything is relaxed and happy. It represents the goal you should set yourself.

Similarly, your dreamscape could represent your life. The roads you travel in your dream may be a metaphor for the roads you travel through life. The twists, turns, and obstacles are the difficulties you encounter in ordinary life. A fork in the road or a crossroads may represent a difficult decision you have to make.

If your dream has a symbolic meaning it is probably not a dream that recalls a past life. However, do not necessarily dismiss it. It could be saying to you, "What you are experiencing now is just like the time you were at this place…." "This place" may be somewhere from a past life.

Foreign Dreamscapes

When you dream of a strange land do not assume that this is of a past life. Again it may be a symbol for problems that you are experiencing in this life. To dream of being in a foreign country may indicate that you are experiencing something unfamiliar in your waking life. Foe example, you may have recently changed jobs or may be behaving differently from your usual routine.

These dreams are often accompanied by uncomfortable feelings of loss or anxiety. Your dream may be telling you that you are not ready to leave your present life behind. Perhaps you are not prepared to deal with the circumstances that are currently dominating your life. Everything feels "foreign" to you. You are a stranger in a strange land.

Foreign dreamscapes can also represent opportunity and excitement. Positive feelings about your dreamscape may show that you are enjoying new opportunities that have been presented in your life. You may have a new job opening; new opportunities may be coming your way.

Again this dreamscape may be a symbol of your life. Despite its strangeness, it is not necessarily about a life long ago. It is most likely to be a metaphor for your life.

OBE Dreamscapes

Many people, including myself, believe that they have left their body during sleep. A body of light leaves the physical body and can travel across the landscape of the Earth and also to the stars and heavenly spheres. This is a very commonly reported experience.

Dreamscapes you experience during this state of awareness could be real places. Out of body experiences (OBE's) may also give you access to the halls of learning in the heavenly planes. Some have called this level of vibration the "akashic record," which contains the "recording" of everything that has ever happened. It could be described as God's memory. If this information can be accessed, your past lives and the past lives of anyone can be accessed. The psychic "sleeping prophet" Edgar Cayce believed that much of the information he gave came from his ability to access the akashic record of the past lives of the people who consulted him.

The akashic record is a plane of existence storing the memories and knowledge of everything that has happened. It is like a cosmic Internet that contains the imprints of everything that has existed on the material and spiritual planes. Tune into the akashic record and you will be able to watch dinosaurs walk the earth, see the Fall of Troy, or hear Lincoln deliver the Gettysburg Address.

SHOWBIZ PAST LIVES

Many top show biz stars believe that they lived before. Many of the roles they play may reflect the characters they were in past lives:

- **Shirley MacLaine:** She is perhaps the most well known reincarnationalist. She believes she was a maidservant in ancient Egypt and a model for Toulouse-Lautrec in France.
- **Sylvester Stallone:** The star of *Rambo* and other blockbusters is convinced he lived during the French Revolution. He believes he was guillotined.
- **Engelbert Humperdinck:** This singer believes he was a Roman Emperor in a past life.
- **Tina Turner:** This singer is so convinced she has lived before, she searched for evidence of a past life in Egypt. Her quest began after a Californian psychic told her she was the reincarnation of Hatshepsut a woman pharaoh of ancient Egypt.
- **John Travolta:** The star of the films *Saturday Night Fever* and more recently *Phenomenon* believes he was an actor in a past life, perhaps even Rudolf Valentino.
- **Martin Sheen:** Sheen is a firm believer in reincarnation and believes that families do not come together by chance. "Our children," he says, "come to us to make up for indiscretions in

past lives. They are holdovers from lifetimes we have not solved."

SOURCE: Reincarnation: amazing cases from around the world. Roy Stemman. Piatkus. London 1997

Past Life Dreamscapes

Once you have eliminated dreamscapes that have clear symbolic meaning you are left with a number of locations that cannot be explained. There's a certain "grand dream" feeling that often accompanies these dreams. Even as the dream is taking place you may have a feeling of awe and wonder. You awaken knowing that this dream is very special and that it relates to something about your distant past. There's an inescapable feeling that the dream is about a past life.

In most cases it is impossible to prove beyond doubt that a dream relates to a past life experience. How much easier it would be if you could simply dream all the facts then prove them with public records of births, marriages, and deaths. I have listed some intriguing examples of past life cases in the sidebar to this section. However, in most cases dream revelations about past lives are likely to remain unproven. I suppose it finally comes down to a gut feeling, an unshakable knowing that comes from deep within you.

There are certain dreams you are likely to have had that cannot be explained away as symbolism, metaphor, or allegory. In my own dream records I have cases I am convinced are about past lives. For example I had many dreams about being a shaven-headed monk when I was a child. At the time I had never heard of Tibet or the doctrine of reincarnation. In particular I would have a dream about walking around in a circle on what looked like high walled tower . Together with other monks, I chanted mantras. The scenery was spectacular. I would awaken feeling tremendously inspired. I have also had recurring dreams about dying of exposure near a dried-up riverbed, which I now believe to be the source of the Yellow River in Mongolia, a place where there were many Tibetan monasteries. (My wife often jokes that I feel the cold too much for an incarnation of a Tibetan.)

Although I do not follow the Buddhist way today, I feel that Tibetan wisdom and teachings still influence me. It may explain why I was born with mediumistic powers and how easily I grasp Tibetan Buddhist and Bon ideas that many people find hard to understand.

Perhaps the strangest past life dream I had was about being chased from behind by raging dogs. A small group of people and I are near a castle. Our way is blocked by a moat. As the dogs catch up with us, soldiers start attacking us from behind with swords. There is a lot of noise and commotion. I can smell fire and blood. I feel a terrible pain in the back of my neck. There is searing pain, then nothing.

When I met my wife, Jane, who is also a medium, we talked about our dreams and were amazed to discover that we had this same dream in common--right down to the smallest detail. Neither of us knows the historical time period it relates to, although it hints at the Medieval era, when mediums were persecuted as witches. It could of course all be fantasy, except that Jane, myself, and our daughter Danielle each have the same brown birth mark at the top of the neck just under the hairline. Perhaps we three are beheaded soulmates?

Why don't we remember our past lives?

Spontaneous recall of past lives may be a rather dubious privilege. Suppose you were now able to have unfettered access to all your past life memories and were to discover that you were one of the worst monsters in history. What if you discovered that you were Genghis Khan, Hitler, or Stalin? Worse, perhaps, you realize you have spent lifetimes as a child abuser or village idiot. How would you feel? How would you deal with the horror and belated remorse? You would probably feel so depressed and discouraged, you would have no strength to keep on.

Moreover, imagine how much karma your life now and in the future would be subject to. You would have a mountain of misfortune to deal with. How could you deal with it? Perhaps you would live in fear of retribution for past sins. You would probably feel hopelessness, guilt, and shame and find it tremendously difficult to get on with your life. People don't like to remember things that are unpleasant or evil.

Fortunately cosmic law protects you with forgetfulness and gives you a second chance. People need to be protected even from comparatively innocuous past lives. Take for example the story of Shanti Devi, in the sidebar near this section. Twenty-five years after the events described, a reporter sought out Shanti to ask her about the case. She was working a quiet life as a government employee. She was not keen to talk about the case. "I do not wish to revive my past lives, either this one or my previous existence in Muttra," she confessed. "It has been very difficult for me to bury my desire to return to my family. I do not want to open that closed door again."

CASE STUDY: Shanti Devi

One of the best-known cases of reincarnation is that of Jumari Shanti Devi, who was born in Delhi, India, in 1926. When she was seven, she told her mother that she had lived before in a town called Muttra. She explained that she had been married to a man called Kedarnath.

"He lives in Muttra. Our house is yellow stucco with large arched doors and latticework windows. Our yard is large and filled with marigolds and jasmine. Great bowers of scarlet bougainvilleas climb over the house. We often sit on the veranda watching our little son play on the tile floor. Our sons are still there with their father."

During the next two years her memories of her previous life increased. She told the family doctor that her name had been Ludgi. Soon she was telling her parents everything about her previous life.

When she was nine, a Mr Lal came to the door to discuss business with her father. She immediately recognized the stranger as someone she knew in her past life. "Mother! This is a cousin of my husband!" she exclaimed." He lived not far from us in Muttra and then moved to Delhi. I am so happy to see him!"

The man did live in Muttra. He agreed that his cousin's wife, Ludgi, had died 10 years earlier. Eventually, Shanti was taken to visit her family from her previous life. When she first saw the husband she recognized him immediately and flung herself into his arms. She called him by her own pet names and used endearing phrases which only he and his wife had known.

Shanti was able to direct the carriage to Ludgi's house in Muttra and identified her father-in-law sitting in front of it. She also recognized her two eldest children and knew their names, but not the youngest, whose birth had cost Ludgi her life. Next, they visited Ludgi's elderly mother Desh Gupta. Shanti told her that there used to be a well on the property and indicated the correct place it had been. Kedarnath then asked what Ludgi had done with several rings she had been given shortly before her death. She explained that she had hidden them in a pot in the garden of the old home. An investigating committee later excavated these.

You may ask yourself the question: "What have I done in a past life to deserve this suffering?" But you forget that it was you who chose to take on the life you have today. Perhaps in a past life you were a king, queen, president, or rich person. At the end of your last life you may have decided that seeking fame, power, privilege, or wealth are futile pursuits. Perhaps you enjoyed your status and came to the end of that experience. You learned what you needed to know.

When you last died you passed down the tunnel of light and let go of everything you were. What survived is the essential you, the part of you that the Hindu philosopher Sri Aurobindo called the psychic being. After a period of rest in the afterlife, you made the decision to take another earthly life. This time you choose new lessons to learn based on your karma and desires. You can only be free of rebirth once your path is set to the Divine.

Your task now is to fulfil the destiny you set for yourself. You must work to learn the sometimes-hard lessons you have set. You do not remember your past lives because these memories might hamper your spiritual progress. They could cause feelings of guilt or yearning for experiences past.

The memories in your unconscious are immortal. Although the memory of your past lives has vanished from your mind, if the appropriate brain cells were awakened you would be able to remember everything. Very often, these silent areas of the mind are opened during sleep and the memories awaken during dreams.

The habits you cultivated in past lives have created your physical, mental, and emotional makeup in this life. You also bring forward into this life your past karma which determines the kind of physical form you will have as well as your personality traits. Even your sex is determined by your self-chosen tendencies in previous lives.

By knowing your past lives, you can gain an understanding of yourself and the traits that are influencing the course of your life. Most people never analyze themselves, so they are continually stuck in a rut of established behavior. They are guided by their likes and dislikes, all of which are habits brought forward from previous lives.

The objective of a self-aware person is to be in control and not to be at the mercy of his own tendencies. Knowing about your past lives can help you establish new habits and help you get out of physical, emotional, mental, and spiritual ruts. Few people try consciously to change themselves. They are stuck with preconceptions that they are sinners or weak or are temperamental, and so on. These are all habits established in past lives.

USING PAST LIFE RECALL TO IMPROVE YOURSELF

Most people who go to fortune-tellers to discover their past lives want to be flattered. They don't want to hear that they were once evil or dull individuals. They want to be heroic figures, a great king or queen, a martyr to the French Revolution, a great sage, or famous in some way. Often the incarnations they imagine reflect their wishes and hopes, acting as an escape from their dull and banal lives. Unfortunately many false prophets tell people what they want to hear, and the grip of the illusion becomes stronger. In my own work as a Spiritualist medium, I have met a plentiful supply of ex-Nefertitis, pharaohs, Nelsons, and Queens of Sheba. It always surprises me that these great souls now incarnate as such dull and tedious individuals in this life.

If you were to truly remember who you are, you might realize that you are an immortal soul. You are Spirit and not the temporal being that walks this earth. During the day, you are tricked by your habits and false memory into believing that you are this limited physical being. However, during sleep you are free to unite with the totality of yourself. You are reminded that you are a formless Divine being. You lose all consciousness of your body and form and are reminded that you are Spirit. Your nature is bliss.

The insight that your dreams give you into your past lives can be used to bring you closer to this realization. If you remember past lives that make you feel ashamed, learn from this and rid yourself of these qualities in this life. Similarly if your past-life recall reveals good qualities in a former life, reintroduce them into your life today. Most of all let your life be filled with happy memories from both this life and the ones before. This will keep you healthy and happy. And in particular, use your knowledge go beyond mortal consciousness. You have come down from the Spirit to this limited world of flesh. There is no end to your consciousness. You have memories of lives that stretch back into the vast eons of time. It is all there within you. A time will come when you no longer have to make an effort to remember anything. It is all there within you in your omnipresent intuition.

Using dreams to recognize souls you have known in a past incarnation

Why is it that you feel an immediate and deep harmony with some people when you meet them for the first time? Yet you work with others day after day for years and never really get to know them. The reason might be that the ones you feel an immediate kinship with, you knew in a past life. Seeing them again rekindles your friendship, which continues to grow in this lifetime. Friendship is the highest relationship because it is born of free choice. Marriages that have friendship as their foundation are stronger than those based on wealth, sex, or emotion. To be a friend to all is the unfolding of God's unconditional love. Friendship can bind people together over the centuries.

If you discuss your dreams with your partner, you may find that throughout your lifetime you have held dreams in common. Of course, you may not have been friends in a past life. Sometimes your karma brings you together so you can sort out your differences. However, knowledge of dreams about your past lives will help you resolve your difficulties and generate true friendship and love. Relationships should be seen as mutual spiritual work. They should be based on soul qualities, not worldly qualities or attractions of the flesh. If you base all your friendships and relationships on spiritual values, you will attract another spiritual friend, for God now holds you in His hands.

Your dreams reveal a great deal about past relationships with people you know now. When friends, family, and enemies appear in your dreams, make a note in your dream diary. What do you remember about the setting and era in which the dream is set? Of course, in most instances your friends will be dream symbols representing the way you feel about your life at the moment. For example, friends of the same sex can represent your shadow self, the aspects of your personality you have refused to acknowledge consciously. The friendly nature suggests that you are prepared to integrate this neglected part with yourself. Dreams about family members can also represent parts of your personality. For example, if you dream about your mother this could symbolize the motherly side of yourself, the part of you that wants to nurture and protect. A dream about your father may represent your outward going nature and the dynamic forces within you. Even if this is not the case in reality, your dreams will cast the characters from your life in mythic, archetypal roles.

But some dreams are not symbolic. They are direct references to past incarnations. If you compare your dream notes with those of people you like the most, you may find that you have many dreams in common. As you dig deeper, you may discover that some of these dreams are too specific to be the result of chance alone. The details may reveal periods in history and lives you had in common. By working in this way you can prove to yourself that you are not a victim of your own fantasy but that your past life memories can be substantiated through others. You may also discover that groups of your friends have dreams in common.

Group souls

A particularly interesting case of group incarnation was penned by Arthur Guirdham in his book *The Cathars and Reincarnation*. This is a factual record of a woman who, through dreams and waking impressions, remembered her previous life in the 13th century. She was burned for heresy around 1244. Guirdham, the author, was a doctor of medicine and a psychiatrist, and was trained to distinguish between fact and fantasy. At first, he was skeptical when the woman insisted she was the incarnation of a heretic Cathar who lived in France during the 13th century. However, her dreams revealed knowledge of the times that only a specialist scholar would know. Guirdham decided to investigate the places mentioned and the historic records to check the patient's statements.

Remarkably, he discovered that his woman's dreams gave accurate historical information that she could not have known. Her dreams were full of precise detail about the Cathars. She asserted that Cathar priests wore blue, not black, which proved to be correct. She was able to place accurately in their family and social relationships people who were not historical characters but who, with a great deal of research, could be traced through public records. But it was the little thing that gave weight to her story. For example, her dreams revealed that she had given her lover loaf sugar when he was ill. Careful research revealed that loaf sugar was regarded as a medicine at the time.

As Guirdham continued his research, he discovered that he too could retrieve memories from an incarnation as a Cathar. As the book unfolds, the dreams reveals a whole network of people connected by a common spiritual lineage from the when the Inquisition wiped out this pious group of Cathars. Centuries later, they were to be reborn together again, and the past forgotten, except in dreams.

How far back can you remember?

Studies of people put under hypnosis show that the mind has a remarkable ability to record huge amounts of information. Many psychologists believe that the brain may be able to remember every detail of everything that has ever happened to it. All the memories are there, most people just lack the ability to access the information. Dreams are a doorway to this treasure-trove of forgotten wisdom.

As has been mentioned earlier, mystics believe that a repository of memory exists that is separate from any one of us. It is called the akashic record. Much of the information you access about your past lives may come from this source. However you also have personal memories. Like the akashic record, the amount of knowledge that your mind can store may be limitless. I have had very strange dreams about what appear to be Neolithic or Stone Age times. Moreover, places like Stonehenge and the other ancient megaliths fill me with a mixture of excitement, peace, and dread that is difficult to explain. Dreams appear to reach back in times to scenarios with a familiar feel, to places I feel that I once knew. Some of my dreams are even set in jungle or tribal settings.

If you work with your ability at dream recall over many years, you will access the deepest buried memories from the unconscious. Not only will you awaken your memory of human lives but animal lives as well.

Dream memories of animal lives

More people are alive today than at any other time in human history. Given that reincarnation is true, where did all these new souls come from? The truth is, there aren't enough human souls to go around. It's a significant fact that as the human population is increasing, the animal population is decreasing. The conclusion seems to be that animal souls are all reincarnating as human beings. Carefully observe your fellow humans and you will soon see the hidden animal spirit expressing itself.

All of us, say the gurus, have had previous lives as animals and have gradually climbed the spiritual ladder of evolution to attain our present human life. It is a fact that our archaic animal past is still deeply ingrained in our everyday behavior. For "new" humans, the former animal lives are particularly apparent. First-time humans may still behave like animals: We talk of a person acting like a rat, eating like a pig, or singing like a canary. Hidden within these similes are references to previous lives.

Dreams can occasionally reveal memories from your animal past. You may have direct memories, but it is more likely that they are ingrained in your instinctive behavior. Your instinctive fears, which often appear in dreams, may also say a great deal about your former animal lives. For example, you may have a fear of snakes or spiders. Perhaps the thought of a tiger or a crocodile fills you with dread because these animals may have taken you life in a past animal incarnation.

Now have some fun. Answer the following questions to see what animal you were in a past life:

Are you a vegetarian?
Most animals are herbivorous. With so many animal souls incarnating it's not surprising that vegetarianism has become fashionable. You are most likely to have been an animal such as a cow, buffalo, antelope, or perhaps even a squirrel. Avoid people who like to eat nearly raw steaks or meatballs - these people are from another species entirely and may do you harm. Your dreams may reveal a fear of being chased.

Do you feel safer when surrounded by friends?
A "yes" answer shows that your animal lineage is with herding animals such as sheep and with species that seek safety in numbers. Your past life may have been within a school of fish, a flock of birds, or herd of wildebeests. If you were a fish, you may have dreams about breathing underwater.

Do you like to go on the prowl?
Gangs of thugs of course originate from pack animals such as wolves, and it's possible that many great generals were wolves in their former lives. There is no greater compliment to a Hell's Angel than to call him the leader of the pack. Today hunting grounds are clubs and bars. These are the places where latter-day wolves like to prowl. Your dreams may be filled with violent images.

Do you feel sleepy in winter?
You are remembering the time when you used to hibernate. Many fish, amphibians, reptiles, and mammals such as hedgehogs and bats from the colder regions of the world sleep through the winter months. You lose weight during winter, prefer colder climates, and don't feel quite yourself until spring. Your dreams may feature caves or subterranean passageways.

What animal do you look like?
What animal features do you see when you look in the mirror? Some

people have protruding teeth like a camel, tiny mouselike eyes, or a mane of lion's hair. Have you a square-set face like a bull or a thin storklike appearance? Look for some time and you'll suddenly see your animal face staring back at you. Your dreams about the animals you like may reveal your own past.

What does your body language say about your animal spirit?

Because of its instinctive origins, body language reveals a great deal about animal past lives. For example you may stand proud like a bull or swivel your head like a prairie dog watching for predators. You may strut like a peacock or scurry along like a mouse. People who blink a lot may be incarnations of owls! Could it be that your dreams of flying are an actual memory from long ago?

What do your habits say about your animal past?

Primitive peoples say that our totem animal dream soul influences our habits. A woman who stuffs her handbag full of junk may be displaying the hoarding instincts of a hamster or even the maternal behavior of a kangaroo. Nail biting is a throwback to the days when you had claws, and a love of swimming shows your aquatic past life. Dreams that reveal phobias about snakes, spiders, or birds also reflect ancient animal fears..

7 SEEING THE FUTURE

The future belongs to those who believe in their dreams
Eleanor Roosevelt (1884-1962)
Wife of US President Franklin D Roosevelt

The idea that dreams can predict the future has captivated the imagination for thousands of years. The ancient Egyptians, Greeks, and Romans believed that the gods could communicate to them through dreams that often contained prophecies of the future. Some of the most well-known examples or dream precognition are in the Bible. The Book of Genesis tells about the dreams of Joseph, son of Jacob. Joseph told his brothers: "we were binding sheaves in the field, and lo, my sheaf arose and stood upright; and behold, your sheaves gathered around it, and bowed down to my sheaf; …. Behold, the sun moon and eleven stars were bowing down to me."

Outraged at Joseph's proclamations his eleven brothers kidnapped him and he was sold into slavery in Egypt. In prison, Joseph interpreted the dreams of his fellow inmates, predicting that one would be freed but another hanged. Two years later the freed man told the pharaoh of Joseph's remarkable ability to interpret prophetic dreams. He was summoned to court to explain the meaning of a dream that had confounded all the wise men of Egypt. The pharaoh described his dream. He stood on the bank of the Nile and watched "seven fat kine" (cows) emerge from the river. The fat cows grazed contentedly by the shoreline but "seven other kine followed them; poor and very ill-favored and lean-fleshed, much as I have never seen in Egypt. And the ill-famed kine did eat up the fat kine." The pharaoh awoke, but later the dream continued, showing him seven full heads of grain being eaten by seven withered heads of grain.

Joseph understood the dream. It was a warning from God to say that

Egypt would enjoy seven years of plenty followed by seven years of famine. The pharaoh believed Joseph and gave orders that enough grain be stored to last through the seven lean years.

Egypt and the Middle East were indeed wracked with the predicted famine. When Joseph's father and his eleven brothers came to Egypt to buy grain they met Joseph, now elevated to an important position as reward for his insight. The brothers recalled his prophecy from long ago that his father, mother, and brothers would honor him: "Behold, the sun, moon, and eleven stars were bowing down to me."

Throughout the Bible, many prophecies come from dreams. In the Old Testament God granted Solomon the gift of wisdom in a dream, Daniel predicted the destiny of king Nebuchadnezzar, and Jacob dreamed of a ladder of angels when God announced that Jacob's descendants would spread throughout the world like the stars in the sky. In the New Testament, the apostle Matthew wrote that four angels spoke to Joseph in a dream and that Joseph's virgin wife Mary would bear a divine child. Similarly, another dream warned Joseph and Mary of the cruel edict of Herod enabling them to flee to Egypt with the Divine Child.

Although the philosopher Aristotle argued that precognitive dreams were impossible, he was unusual for his time. Most ancient Greeks believed dreams foretold the future. They consulted soothsayers at the temple of Apollo for interpretations of dream portents. The Romans also believed that dreams could foretell the future. If Julius Caesar had been less skeptical about them, he might have listened to the warnings about his assassination that Calpurnia, his wife, received in a dream.

The course of history has been influenced by precognitive dreams. As a young man, Oliver Cromwell had a dream in which a huge female figure drew back the curtains around his bed. She told him he would be the greatest man in England, but not the king. The impossible came true after the English Civil War when Cromwell signed King Charles' death warrant and became Lord Protector of England--the most powerful man in the land.

The military campaigns of the French emperor Napoleon were often changed because of messages he received in dreams. Similarly, Otto von Bismarck, the militaristic German chancellor, claimed that a prophetic dream convinced him to continue his 1866 campaign against the Austrians.

Abraham Lincoln assigned prophetic value to certain dreams and dreamed of his own death in 1865. In the dream, he wandered around a "death like" White House and could hear the distant sound of sobbing. The sound led him to the East Room where he saw a corpse laid out. Its face was covered and the body wrapped in funeral vestments. He asked the sobbing mourners who the dead person and was told "the president was killed by an assassin." A few days later the dream came horribly true when

John Wilkes Booth assassinated Abraham Lincoln in a theater.

Many contemporary examples of dreams that come true are sent to me through my newspaper columns. Ordinary people who make no claim to special powers have written to say that they have seen the future. "I awoke from a bad dream at exactly 9:03. In the dream I saw my father collapse outside the hospital in Glasgow" wrote Pamela from Knightswood. "Exactly two months later at 9:03 a.m. my father collapsed and died at the exact spot that I had dreamt about."

Another account sent to me about of precognition in a dream revealed facts of startling accuracy. "I awoke from a vivid dream and told it to my husband so that I could put it into my diary later. The dream was not pictorial; it was auditory. I had heard a name, Neville, not that unusual, but I didn't know anyone by that name. I had also dreamed of the poem "Upon Westminster Bridge," by the poet William Wordsworth.

"Three months later I joined a discussion group and was introduced to a Neville Westbridge. We became good friends and his ideas had a very important influence on my philosophy of life. My husband has always been very skeptical about precognition but the accuracy of this dream has made him change his tune."

Some people believe that seership is an inherited gift passed down through families and even racial groups. When a Gypsy girl called at Mrs. Hollings house in County Durham she was amazed to hear how much the Gypsy knew about her and her family. "She knew that my husband had bad legs and went on to predict that my son was engaged to a girl with the initial M but would marry a girl with the initial S. Their firstborn would be twins."

The Gypsy's prediction came true to the letter.

Often the dreams sent to me contain foreboding messages or give warnings: "I was working on an oil rig 80 miles out in the Arabian Gulf. Because we were working 12 hour shifts most of us went to bed early," says JW from Portsmouth UK "On a Thursday night at 7:35 p.m. I awoke from a bad dream. I had been floating about 100 feet in the air above a street near my home watching a car traveling along a dual carriageway. Without stopping, it drove straight across a roundabout and hit another vehicle. I sensed rather than saw that the guilty driver was my father.

I told my friend about the dream.

A week later I was flown home. My father had had an accident in exactly the way my dream had revealed. He told me that as he was driving he started thinking about me in Bahrain and wondering how I was getting on. Suddenly he hit a car at the roundabout. Luckily nobody was hurt. The time was 4:35 p.m. Between Bahrain and the UK is a three-hour time difference in the summertime. The accident happened at exactly the time I dreamed it."

PARANORMAL RESEARCH

I believe everybody that has psychic power lying dormant in the mind. Scientists call these powers Extra Sensory Perception (ESP). ESP subdivides into telepathy (communicating by thought), clairvoyance (seeing events without using the five senses), psychokinesis (influencing matter by thought, i.e. spoon bending), and precognition (seeing the future)

Psychic powers have been researched since the 1930s, when Professor J. B. Rhine at Duke University in North Carolina made a systematic study in the laboratory. He presented his evidence by the statistical analysis of card-guessing games. Rhine discovered that many students randomly selected from the university campus could predict which cards would come next in a randomly shuffled pack of Zener cards. Their scores were far above what would be expected by chance alone.

Extensive sleep experiments were conducted to test whether ESP is present in dreams. Experiments were designed to see if telepathy could take place in dreams. An Italian psychic researcher named G B Ermacora at the turn of the 20th century undertook some of the first trials. These marked the first serious attempt at inducing dream telepathy with a pre-selected sender and receiver.

Other interesting experiments were conducted in the 1940s by William Daim, a Viennese psychologist. Sitting in a closed room at a considerable distance from the sleeping receiver, he randomly chose an envelope from a pile on a table. In each were "target" pictures. Many of the dreams of his receivers contained similar images to those he had "sent" by telepathy.

The most extensive research into dream ESP was conducted in the late '60s and early '70s by a research team led by Montague Ullman and Stanley Krippner at the Maimonides Medical Center in Brooklyn, New York. They used similar techniques to William Daim but had the advantage of being able to wire up their subjects to EEG machines that could detect changes in brain patterns and the onset and ending of REM periods. The best results were obtained by selecting images and paintings with strong emotional overtones. They observed that if a subject's dream "is vivid, colored, and somewhat puzzling to the dreamer and does not 'fit' into his dream pattern or reflect recent activity, then we can be alerted to the possibility that the dream is being influenced by ESP."

In their book entitled Dream Telepathy, Ullman and Krippner wrote, "Perhaps our most basic finding is the scientific demonstration of Freud's statement 'Sleep creates favorable conditions for telepathy.'"

The Maimonides team also made extensive research into dreams and precognition. One of their most gifted subjects was an Englishman named Malcolm Bessent who had scored high in telepathy experiments and had been used for a number their of high-profile dream experiments. One of their most successful experiments in dream precognition lasted 16 nights, with each experiment covering two nights. On the first night, Bessent would attempt to dream about which target picture would be chosen for the following night. On the second night he would see the target and try to dream about it. On the third night a new target would be chosen and the sequence repeated.

The Maimonides team found that Bessent had, on the eight precognitive dream nights, scored seven hits. On the eight control nights, his dream images bore little or no resemblance to the target pictures. The odds of this happening by change were an amazing 1,000 to 1.

Research into ESP continues to this day and now uses video clip "targets" instead of static imagery. ESP experiments have even been done in space. It seems ironic that experiments in precognition, which started in the ancient Greek temple of Apollo, should be secretly carried out on its namesake, the Apollo 14 space mission, by astronaut Edgar D Mitchell in the 1960s. Experiments in precognition have been going on for centuries. Many people have this ESP gift. Perhaps you are one of them.

OTHER THEORIES ABOUT DREAM PREMONITION

In your normal waking life, you take it for granted that time goes in a straight direction, like an arrow pushing ever onward. It doesn't go backward, sideways, or do anything silly. It goes from the past through the present and into the future. Could it be that when you go to sleep and dream, strange things happen to time? How would it be if time did not behave in the ways you have become accustomed in your waking life? You are aware of the past and the present, but is it not possible that your consciousness could extend into the future also. Perhaps one of the reasons you cannot remember your dreams is that they exist in another time frame or give you access to another dimension and created memories that are hard to bring forward into your ordinary world.

Many great thinkers have wrestled with the enigma of time. Saint Augustine, Galileo, Sir Isaac Newton, Albert Einstein, and Stephen Hawking have failed to explain it. The most recent theories about time reveal some very strange scenarios. For example, it is believed that if it were possible to travel between two black holes in space, you would move through time. Scientists now talk about hyperspace and cosmic wormholes that tunnel through space-time leading from one region to another. Particle physics also has discovered strange subatomic particles that appear to travel backward in time or appear to be in two places at once. Einstein has also shown that time is relative. Time for one observer may be completely different from the time of another. "When you sit with a nice girl for two hours, you think it's only a minute" said Einstein. "But when you sit on a hot stove for a minute, you think it's two hours. That's relativity."

If you dream of the future, it may indicate that you are in touch with an alternative reality. That's something J. W. Dunne suspected when he noticed that many of his dreams appeared to foretell the future. Dunne was a distinguished man of science and a professor of mathematics. He noticed that sometimes his dreams took an odd view of time and sometimes included disagreements about time. In one dream, he was convinced it was 4:30 in the afternoon. When he awoke looked at his wrist to check the time but found that his watch was missing. Then he spotted it on his bedroom cabinet. It had stopped at 4:30.

Dunne was sufficiently intrigued by what happened to keep a dream diary. He kept detailed records and would sometimes compare dreams with friends. Applying the methodology that he learned from mathematics his experiments convinced him that his dreams were foreseeing the future. He found also that prophetic thoughts could be engendered in the waking mind if kept in a state of receptivity. Furthermore, he suspected that most people had the ability to predict future events.

In 1927, he published his conclusions in his book *An Experiment with Time*. It became a bestseller, caused great controversy, and is still the center of much debate among contemporary researchers. Dunne's book challenged the notion that time traveled in a straight line with a definite past, present, and future. He argued that his dreams proved that time was not a continuum. He believed that if time was a fourth dimension, then the passage of time must itself take time. Therefore, if time took time, there had to be a time outside time. He called this "Time 2." "Time," he said "is not a straight line, like a stretched cord; it is more like a tangled skein of wool."

Most of our life we live in "Time 1," which is synonymous with the passing ordinary moments of everyday life. But during sleep a part of our personality (Observer 2) can slip into this other dimension of time and experience events in the future that are communicated to our ordinary self (Observer 1). In other words, past, present, and future exist as one, and we only understand it as a series of events because our consciousness organizes it in this way. Dunne concluded that under certain circumstances, past, present, and future events were accessible to us. During sleep, your rationality and logic take a back seat, so you access multi-levels of time in your dreams. During dreams, you can enter this forth dimension of space-time. Hence, dreams can not only be about the past and present but about a pre-existent future. Just as you can have memories of the past, so too you can have memories of the future.

So is Dunne saying that the future is predetermined? We are used to determining the outcome of our lives, and society is based on self-determination of the future. It is the backbone of the American Dream: everyone can progress through effort and ambition. A future that is completely pre-determined runs against everything we hold to be true. If there's nothing we can do about our destiny then why bother trying to change things? It's fate, and we're stuck with it.

Some of Dunne's dreams of the future suggest that there is predetermination, particularly when the dreams concern newsworthy events. For example, while stationed as a soldier in South Africa during the spring of 1902 Dunne dreamed he was on an island in imminent peril from a volcano. Later he was seized by a frantic desire to save the islanders, believing that 4,000 people were in danger. Throughout the dream, he recalled trying to convince incredulous French authorities to remove the islanders to safety.

Sometime after the dream, at 8 o'clock Thursday morning, May 1902, Mount Pelee erupted, destroying St Pierre, the main trading island of the French colony Martinique in the West Indies. Dunne read about it in the Daily Telegraph. His dream had come horribly true except that his figures were wrong: 40,000 people had died, not 4,000, as his dream had predicted.

This dream clearly showed that a disaster was going to take place and there was very little anyone could do about it. However, Dunne had other dreams that did not necessarily predict the future but gave warnings that allowed him to avoid catastrophe. On one occasion in 1904 while staying in a hotel in Aachensee, Austria, Dunne dreamed he was being chased across a field by a wild horse:

"I dreamed one night that I was walking down a sort of pathway between two fields, separated from the latter by high iron railings, eight or nine feet high [2.4 or 2.7 m high], on each side of the path. My attention was suddenly attracted to a horse in the field on my left. It had apparently gone mad, and was tearing about, kicking and plunging in a most frenzied fashion. I cast a hasty glance backward and forward along the railings to see if there were any openings by which the animal could get out. Satisfied that there was none, I continued on my way. A few moments later I heard hoofs thundering behind me. Glancing back I saw, to my dismay, that the brute had somehow got out after all, and was coming full tilt after me down the pathway. It was a full-fledged nightmare- and I ran like a hare. Ahead of me the path ended at the foot of a flight of wooden steps rising upward. I was striving frantically to reach these when I awoke."

The next day Dunne went fishing with his brother near the local river and the events of the dream began to unfold. A horse that they could see across the river was behaving just as in the dream. Dunne could see the same wooden steps but the fences were only four or five feet high. Also, the fields were ordinary small fields whereas in the dream they had been parklike expanses. Similarly the horse was small and unlike the rampaging monster of the dream. Dunne told his brother about the dream and said "At any rate, this horse cannot get out" and they continued with their fishing.

But there was no dodging fate. To the amazement of both men the horse suddenly got out, plunged into the river, and galloped toward the wooden steps, coming straight at them. They ran 30 yards (27 m) or so from the bank and turned around. The horse stopped, looked at them, and galloped off down the road.

Clearly, Dunne's dream had come true, well, almost true. The fact is, his dream contained many things that were not precise. This is often the case with dreams about future events. They reveal some of the facts but not all of them. Dunne theorized that dreams of the future are only a sketch of what will happen because people have free will. It's possible to glimpse at future events but since it's also possible to act on what will happen and exercise free will, the dream you initially had of the future may now prove inaccurate.

My own view is that the future is like a landscape. What you see in dreams are the roads and pathways ahead. You can travel across that landscape any way you please. You may choose a hard road or an easy road. If you see an obstacle you can travel over it or move around it. Destiny is like the landscape, your journey is your free will and your dreams of the future are maps that guide you.

DO YOU DREAM OF THE FUTURE?
Are you a secret psychic?

I believe everyone is psychic to some extent, but in normal waking life the rational mind pushes the subtle impressions away. During sleep the rational mind is less active and psychic abilities are able to come alive. You have incredible powers locked within your mind just waiting to be triggered! Some are born with them, others develop them, but everyone has them. Psychic powers are part of ancient survival skills dating back to before the invention of language.

Our prehistoric ancestors sensed the atmosphere of good or hostile places, could orient themselves without maps, and could share thoughts by telepathy.

Even today, some cultures, such as the Aborigines, retain these skills. You may have even noticed these instinctive ESP abilities in your family pet! ESP is a natural perception but when the rational mind became dominant, somehow these skills were lost. However, buried deep within, everyone has these ancient skills just waiting to be re-animated. You can find out just how much psychic power you possess by taking our specially devised "Psychic IQ Test." You may find that you already have many psychic qualities that you will be able to discover and enhance in your dreams.

My experience as a professional psychic suggests that ESP comes from the irrational, non-verbal, right brain hemisphere, which is also very active during dreams. Scientists know that this is the part of the brain that perceives the world as a whole rather than by dividing it into categories. It may be the source of intuition and psychic awareness. Rationalists and scientists think with their left brain, but artists and psychics think with their right.

For example, when I've demonstrated mind reading on television I've often been able to describe the content of a target location being mentally projected by the audience but I find it infuriatingly difficult to put a name to what I see. ESP is a gut feeling. It comes directly from the intuition and bypasses verbal thinking. If you want to discover your psychic powers you must trust your intuition.

WHAT IS ESP?

The American researcher Joseph Banks Rhine, mentioned briefly earlier in this chapter, is considered the father of scientific paranormal research. In the 1930s at Duke University in Carolina he undertook the first systematic study of the subject and used statistics to quantify his exhaustive tests. Together with his colleague Carl Zener he designed a set of colorful cards of geometric symbols that were used in various card-guessing games. His conclusion was that many people were achieving correct guesses that were far above what would be expect from chance alone. People were receiving information from something other than the known five senses.

Rhine defined this sixth sense as "Extra Sensory Perception" and subdivided it into four basic abilities:

- TELEPATHY: The ability to tune in to the thoughts of others or inject your own thoughts into another's mind. You may experience this if you and someone you know have exactly the same dream.
- CLAIRVOYANCE: The power to see things that are not available to you by the known senses and that are not known by anyone else. A dream about finding a lost object that proves to be correct could be your clairvoyance at work.
- PRECOGNITION: The skill of looking into the future and seeing events before they take place, often through the subconscious when dreaming. Many people believe that dreams reveal facts about the future.
- PSYCHOKINESIS: The ability to use the power of the mind to influence matter or to move objects by thought. This is a rare gift but I have spoken to people who claim they dreamed of moving an object and have then found it in a different room in the morning.

EXPERIMENT: THE PSYCHIC IQ TEST
How psychic are you?

Take this simple questionnaire to find out if you have ESP ability and potential psychic personality traits.

1: When the telephone rings do you:
A: Sometimes know exactly who's unexpectedly calling?
B: Often make a guess at who's calling?
C: Never think about who it may be?

2: When you're angry or upset at work do you:
A: Systematically deal with the task and experience no problems?
B: Notice that occasionally machinery breaks down?
C: Always find that computers crash and photocopiers get stuck?

3: If lost while driving in a strange town do you:
A: Immediately stop the car and consult a map?
B. Drive in what you guess is the general direction?
C: Follow your instincts and drive straight to the address?

4: Are you a person who:
A: Is the life and soul of the party?
B: Likes to express himself but not excessively?
C: Prefers to keep his counsel?

5: When things go very, very wrong do you:
A: Become withdrawn or depressed?
B: Remain anxious but hopeful?
C. Brush off your troubles and maintain a high optimism?

6: When playing board games involving chance do you:
A: Lose despite being careful?
B: Find that you're quite lucky?
C: Enjoy taking risks and feel that you influence the dice in your favor?

7: When you meet someone for the first time do you:
A: Form an immediate assessment of their personality?
B: Guess what they're really like?
C: Reserve judgement?

8: Are you:

A: Logical and systematic in your thinking?
B: Full of good, innovative ideas?
C: Extremely creative and artistic?

9: With newborn babies do you:
A: Leave the care to someone else?
B: Wake from sleep just before they need feeding?
C: Know when an absent baby is upset?

10: When you sleep do you:
A: Dream in color?
B: Never dream?
C: Occasionally dream of events that happen in reality?

11: Do you:
A: Keep an open mind about the existence of ESP?
B. Accept it as completely true?
C. Believe it's all a load of tripe?

12: When you gaze at cumulus clouds do you:
A: See the shapes of faces?
B: See a multitude of changing pictures?
C: See clouds?

ANSWERS
Add up your score and see how psychic you really are:

1: A-3 points, B-2 points, C-1 point
Experiments reveal that telepathy appears to work over any distance. You have a mind to mind link with your friends.

2: A-1 point, B-2 points, C-3 points
Intense moods such as anger can trigger psychokinesis. You may be affecting machinery by the power of your mind.

3: A-1 point, B-2 points, C-3 points
The clairvoyant ability to psychically perceive distant locations was dubbed "remote viewing" by the CIA, which employed psychics to spy on Soviet installations during the Cold War.

4: A-3 points, B-2 points, C-1 point.
Psychic researcher Betty Humphrey from Duke University discovered that extrovert personalities displayed better ESP abilities than introverts.

5: A-1 point, B 2 points, C-3 points
In 1977 researcher John Palmer examined every single published experiment on neuroticism and ESP. He demonstrated that highly neurotic people were poor ESP subjects and optimists scored better results.

6: A 1 point, B 2 points, C 3 points.
It has been shown that gamblers and risk takers display higher ESP abilities. Some may also be able to influence the fall of dice by psychokinesis.

7: A-3 points, B-2 points, C-1 point.
Your gut feelings may be telepathy at work.

8: A-1 point, B-2 points, C-3 points
Imaginative, creative people, and particularly artists, score better in ESP tests than systematic thinkers.

9: A-1 point, B-2 points, C-3 points
A telepathic bond has been proved to be particularly strong between parents and young siblings. Experiments show that a mother's heartbeat increases when her baby wakes and cries, even if in a soundproof room or at another location.

10: A-2 points, B-1 point, C-3 points
People who have intense or lucid dreams often experience precognition.

11: A-2 points, B-3 points, C-1 point.
People who believe in ESP often score better in tests than skeptics. However, some skeptics have ESP ability whether they like it or not and score significantly below chance in card tests. If no ESP were involved they would have only achieve a chance score.

Q12: A-2 points, B-3 points, C: 1 point
Psychic people can often visually project images into random shapes. Scrying (seeing pictures in water or a crystal ball), sand reading, and tea leaf reading all employ this technique.

HOW DID YOU SCORE?

12 to 20 point: You've got far to go. You're as psychic as a bowl of grits.
20 to 28 points: Not bad. You're probably quite psychic.
28 to 36 points: Brilliant! Did you know in advance you were going to take this test?

Dreaming of the Future

Having taken this fun test you may agree that there are many situations where you may have used psychic powers or you may have qualities that give you the opportunity to open your powers in the future. When you first started reading this book you probably thought that you never dreamed or dreamed only occasionally. However, if you've been following the methods outlined in this book, you are likely to be much more aware of your dreams. Discovering your psychic powers is very similar. They're there but you've forgotten about them.

One of the best ways to increase your ability to have prophetic dreams is to become aware of your psychic abilities during normal waking life. Your dreams are responsive and focus on whatever emotional, psychological, or physical state is important to you at the moment. For example, if you are preoccupied with relationship problems your dreams are likely to be about emotional anxieties and sexual issues. To increase your ability to dream about the future you need to think about the future during the day. You could read books about great seers or by good psychics and mediums. Doing this sends a message to your subconscious to help you awaken your intuitive and ESP abilities.

Dream incubation for prophecy

There are many ways to increase your intuitive abilities in everyday life. You can make a start by increasing your awareness of people's vibrations. Can you sense a person's mood when you are with that person? What is your gut feeling? Moods are very easy to pick up by telepathy. You can use this same technique and try to ascertain what mood a person is going to be in before you meet them on a specific day of the week. Try also to guess the future. What TV commercial will come up next? What will be the headline on tomorrow's newspaper? When the telephone rings ask yourself who's calling. Before you open a letter try to sense what it's about. In this way you will increase your sensitivity to vibrations and start to open your latent predictive abilities.

When you first started to recall your dreams I advised you to repeat to yourself affirmations such as: "Tonight I will have a dream". These simple techniques gave you faith in yourself and helped you to believe you could recall your dreams every morning. I'm sure it has worked and you are now you are now either good at recall or, at the very least, can occasionally remember a dream. Similarly, if you have faith in your ability to use psychic powers you will discover them. Belief in the fact that it is possible to see the future will increase your ability to remember dreams about the future. It can be done. You are soon going to use your dreams to look into the future. A conscious effort to have predictive dreams will increase their frequency. It requires patience and practice but is well worth the effort.

Incubating future dream recall

To increase the likelihood that you will remember a dream about the future it is good to repeat an affirmation to yourself during the day. Dream incubation is a powerful method for creating dreams of prophecy and has been used since the time of the ancient Greeks.

You can make up suitable affirmations for yourself or try some of the ones listed here. When you say the affirmation, touch the center of your forehead which is the spiritual "third eye" center. This will help you to be conscious of this important chakra that will be active as you sleep. Here's a few affirmations you can try:

I am a psychic person and open to the guidance I receive.
I know it is possible for me to see into the future.
I give myself permission to remember my dreams of the future.
I welcome the foresight unfolding within me.
I call on the angels to bring me a helpful dream of the future.
The future is calling me.

Prophecies you've already made

If you keep a record of your dreams, you may have noticed already that many of your dreams foretell the future. Other dreams may have appeared to forecast the future but turned out to be incorrect. For example, dreams about death are a very common dream. However, they are rarely a prophecy. In most cases, they are a symbol that represents the way you are feeling. You may feel emotionally overwhelmed by a situation or problem. It is important not to interpret every dream as a prophecy.

Go through your dream diary and highlight with a yellow highlighter any dreams you feel may have either already come true or may be about situations yet to happen. When you read back through your diary, particularly if you keep it for a number of years, it is amazing to see how many dreams contain forecasts of the future.

Most dreams about the future are not dramatic. You are not going to be transformed into the next Nostradamus overnight. Dreams about the future are often subtle and not always easily recognized. You may dream about very ordinary things that come true: something someone says, a letter you will receive, or a person you will meet. You will sometimes wonder why out of all the things you could have foreseen (such as the winner of the Super

Bowl) you see something banal. Nobody knows why this is so. You will often dream junk, but occasionally you will dream about something that may help you a great deal. Some people, such as those who canceled their journey on the Titanic, had their lives saved because they heeded the prompting of a dream.

Keep a diary to write down your dreams. This is the easiest way to remember them. On one side of the page write your dream and on the other write your interpretation.

Go back through the notes in your dream diary and check all your dreams to see if they contain correct premonitions. If you think it is a dream about the future, write "Future?" at the top of the page. If some of the dreams entered in your dream diary are not too personal show the most important ones to a friend or at least tell your friend about them. When your prediction comes true your friend can bear witness to your psychic powers and this will increase your self-confidence and in turn lead to even better results. Belief in yourself is paramount.

Finally don't get too serious and don't worry unduly about your dreams. Dreams are there to help. When a dream makes a prediction it usually also shows ways you can avoid any danger. Dreams reveal the potential future--a future you can change. Dreams are there to help you find the best options for a better future. Listen to their wise advice.

EXPERIMENT: HOW TO DREAM ABOUT THE FUTURE

Have you ever been bombarded with a stream of incredible images as you fall asleep? The colors are so bright and the detail of the images is so vivid, you wonder how your mind can conjure up such amazing scenes. The pictures are strange, surreal, even frightening. They rise and fall in a kaleidoscope of color and form. They stream like a the most complex computer animation. Psychologists call this state of mind hypnagogic dreaming. According to psychics, the imagery that flows at this time can contain symbols and auguries of the future.

Most dreams about the future are of a personal nature rather than about world events. In this experiment, you are going to look into your own future.

Step 1: During the daytime get yourself in the mood for making a prediction. Think about the future and repeat some of the affirmations you read about earlier. Occasionally stop what you are doing and ask yourself: "What will I be doing exactly three weeks from now?" From my own experience and from asking other people who work with prediction it appears that most predictions take about three weeks to come true. The act of asking yourself what you will be doing in three weeks gets you into the mental routine of thinking about the future. You can also look around and ask yourself: "Will anything be different about this place in three weeks' time?" Similarly, you can look at the people around you and say to yourself: "I wonder what they'll be doing in three weeks' time?" Repeatedly doing this will encourage your subconscious to think about the future.

Step 2: Practice guessing the future. As I explained earlier, try guessing which commercial will be on TV next, and so on. What do you think the very last word in this chapter is?

Step 3: Before you go to sleep write a letter to yourself in the future. Ask yourself what advice the future has for you. Having the benefit of foresight, what should you do differently? Pretend there is a real you in the future aware of what you should be doing now who is sending messages back to you. You could also imagine sending messages to the you in the past and giving the right advice at times when things went right for you.

According to Dunne, the self enters a multi-dimensional state of being when you go to sleep, so part of you really is in the future already. Something that Dunne did not say in *An Experiment with Time* but that was revealed in his later writings and interviews was that he believed that people from the spirit world could communicate through multi-dimensional time. (I ask my spirit guide or angel to give me a dream about what I need to know.)

Step 4: Put your letter in an envelope, write your name and address on it, and put it underneath your pillow. This may sound a bit silly but the act of writing the request gives your subconscious mind a command. Putting it in an envelope reinforces this further. And most importantly, since you expect to get a reply from letters you send in real life, so likewise, you anticipate a reply from your subconscious psychic powers. You could reinforce the incubation by: 1. Sending your question by e-mail to yourself last thing at night. 2. As you drop to sleep, imagine that you are speaking to your guardian angel messenger who will return in the night with the answer to your question. 3. Every time the telephone rings, pretend that it is your subconscious with a message about the future.

Step 5: Assuming that your partner has not had you put away, your dreams that night are more likely to contain information about the future. As usual, when you wake up in the morning, write down in the left-hand column of your dream diary everything you can remember about the dream. When you've finished and added the date, title, and so on, add the word "FUTURE," then a short description of the question you asked in your letter. Many of my best predictions are shown to me as I'm falling asleep. If you become conscious of dreaming as you fall asleep, wake yourself up and write down as much as you can remember about the dream. Similarly, if you have mastered the lucid dream techniques from Workshop 4, ask the characters in your dream to tell you about the future.

Step 6: You have already been shown how dreams speak with symbolic language, so don't expect to see the future of your life revealed in a rational way. Your dream may be an allegory of what may happen. Sometimes it's the most uninteresting dreams that contain the most surprising predictions. Look to see if any of your dreams use imagery to represent the future. For example, you dreamed friend was in a car crash. Nothing like that happened but soon afterward she and her husband got a divorce. In retrospect, the dream may have been predicting her emotional crash.

Does the dream contain symbolic messages? You may dream of the actual letter you wrote. Your response to it may indicate the nature of future events. If it makes you feel good, then you feel assured about the future. If the contents cause anxiety, this may indicate that you need to take a more positive attitude. Other things that occur in the dream may represent a reply to the letter under your pillow. Dreaming of receiving a parcel or answering the telephone may represent a message from your unconscious. Similarly, a loud noise such as a bell or siren may symbolize something trying to get your attention. Perhaps there are also symbols of time in your dream--the movement of the sun across the sky, the time of day, a watch, sundial, flowing river, egg timer, and so on. These may hold clues to something your dream is saying about the future.

Consider also what the people in your dream represent about your future. They may represent past situations that remind you of your present and future conditions. Similarly, the landscape may hold clues to what's ahead. An obvious example is if you dream of a road. Where is it leading? Do you see a happy-looking landscape ahead or are their mountains to cross and problems afoot?

Of course, you must be very careful if you decide to work with these future recall methods. Not everything you dream about is going to come true. In most cases the dreams are about your emotional state and reflect your hopes and fears. Don't panic thinking that terrible things are going to happen. Also, remember that dreams tend to exaggerate when they speak about your feelings and also when they give information about your future.

The Dreaming Soul

Remembering your dreams is certainly worthwhile. Your dreams can give you very important insights into all aspects of your life. You've learned to remember dreams to deal with your past, present, and future situations. You now know a great many techniques to help you to get to know yourself better by understanding your hidden hopes, fears, and motives. Dreams enable you get a clearer picture of what it is you want and need from life. They can give you solutions to help you attain your goals.

Modern man has lost touch with his soul. Dreams take you in search of your lost soul and can restore meaning and purpose to life. Dreams help you fill the spiritual void and put you in touch with the higher powers of the mind. They may encourage you to ask some profound questions about life, death, and the purpose of human existence.

Everything needed to make you happy is latent within you. You have incredible innate knowledge, wisdom, energy, and transcendent understanding. It's all there and every night is expressed in dreams. All you need to do is remember.

ABOUT THE AUTHOR

Craig Hamilton-Parker is a British author, television personality and professional psychic medium. He is best known for his TV shows *Our Psychic Family*, *The Spirit of Diana* and *Nightmares Decoded*. On television he usually works with his wife Jane Hamilton-Parker who is also a psychic medium. Their work was showcased in a three part documentary on the BBC called *Mediums Talking to the Dead*.

They now have TV shows in the USA and spend a lot of time demonstrating mediumship around the world.

Born in Southampton UK, Craig was convinced at an early age that he was mediumistic. He became a well known as a platform medium within Spiritualism and in 1994 left his job as advertising executive to become the resident psychic on Channel 4 television's *The Big Breakfast* making predictions for upcoming news stories. He wrote a regular psychic advice column for *The Scottish Daily Record* and regular features for *The Daily Mail*, *Sunday Mirror* and *The People*.

His first book about the psychic genre was published in 1995 and are now published in many languages.

You can find out more and join Craig & Jane's work and Spiritual Foundation at their website: **psychics.co.uk**

YOU MAY ALSO ENJOY THESE BOOKS BY CRAIG HAMILTON-PARKER

BUY FROM PSYCHICS.CO.UK

THE DREAM BOOK TRILOGY

Read all three books in this series. In *Lucid Dreaming and Dream Recall* you are shown how to bring your dreams to life and eventually become a lucid dreamer with the ability to wake up in a dream as it is taking place. In the *Meaning of Dreams and Fantasies* you will learn to interpret and understand your dreams and fantasies. *Mystical Dream Interpretation* explains your psychic dreams and dreams about the future.

MESSAGES FROM THE UNIVERSE

The incredible story of Craig's encounter with the Naadi Oracle of India and how it predicts the future with 100% accuracy – including the future day of his death. Craig tells the story of his encounter with the oracle and writes about the implications of fate and destiny. The book also tells of Craig and his wife Jane's work as a mediumistic couple and how they travel the world giving readings to celebrities and meet holy people as they fulfil the startling predictions made by the oracle.

WHAT TO DO WHEN YOU ARE DEAD

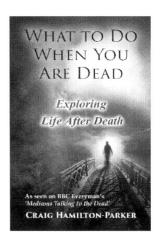

"What to Do When You Are Dead is a landmark book" – Psychic News

Is there life after death? In this book Craig draws on cross cultural beliefs and his own work to describe what life is like in the afterlife. This book will help you to overcome the fear of death and prepare you for the next-life.
Based on extensive research and direct insights the book builds a picture of what the afterlife is like and what life is like on the other side.

PSYCHIC SCHOOL: HOW TO BECOME A PSYCHIC MEDIUM

Filmed over a year in a three part documentary for the BBC, Craig and Jane Hamilton-Parker's psychic students were taught from novices to become mediums capable of working in a theatre. This book expands on the lessons seen in the programs with additional teachings from Craig's thirty years of mediumship. It takes you step-by-step from developing basic psychic powers to becoming a professional medium.

PSYCHIC PROTECTION – SAFE MEDIUMSHIP

If you are a psychic medium or someone who is very sensitive to spiritual vibrations, you may be influenced by the positive or negative energies around you. Through examples from Craig and Jane's files he explains how to combat negative influences, work safely with ghosts, poltergeists, spells and spirits and how to protect your spiritual journey.

ORDER AT: psychics.co.uk

MORE BOOKS BY CRAIG HAMILTON-PARKER

Hamilton-Parker, Craig & Jane (1995) *The Psychic Workbook* Random House ISBN 0-09-179086-7 (Languages: English, Chinese)

Hamilton-Parker, Craig (1996) *Your Psychic Powers* Hodder & Stoughton ISBN 0-340-67417-2 (Languages: English)

Hamilton-Parker, Craig (1999) *Timeless Wisdom of the Tibetans* Hodder & Stoughton ISBN 0-340-70483-7 (Languages: English)

Hamilton-Parker, Craig (1999) *The Psychic Casebook* Blandford/Sterling ISBN 0-7137-2755-1 (Languages: English, Turkish)

Hamilton-Parker, Craig (1999) *The Hidden Meaning of Dreams* Sterling imprint Barnes & Noble ISBN 0-8069-7773-6 (Languages: English, Spanish, Portuguese, Russian, Israeli, Greek Icelandic.)

Hamilton-Parker, Craig (2000) *The Intuition Pack* Godfield Books ISBN 1-84181-007-X

Hamilton-Parker, Craig (2000) *Remembering Your Dreams* Sterling imprint Barnes & Noble ISBN 0-8069-4343-2

Hamilton-Parker, Craig (2000) *Unlock Your Secret Dreams* Sterling imprint Barnes & Noble ISBN 1-4027-0316-3

Hamilton-Parker, Craig (2002) *Fantasy Dreaming Sterling* imprint Barnes & Noble ISBN 0-8069-5478-7

Hamilton-Parker, Craig (2003) *Protecting the Soul* Sterling imprint Barnes & Noble ISBN 0-8069-8719-7

Hamilton-Parker, Craig (2004) *Psychic Dreaming* Sterling imprint Barnes & Noble ISBN 1-4027-0474-7

Hamilton-Parker, Craig (2005) *Opening to the Other Side* Sterling imprint Barnes & Noble ISBN 1-4027-1346-0

Hamilton-Parker, Craig (2010) *What To Do When You Are Dead* Sterling imprint Barnes & Noble ISBN 978-1-4027-7660-1 (Languages: English, Dutch, Portugues

CLAIRVOYANCE SERVICES

Craig & Jane Hamilton-Parker offer psychic and mediumistic readings from their website. They also have an online community where you can ask questions and share your paranormal dreams and psychic insights with like minded people.

Visit: psychics.co.uk

If you would like a reading today you can call their telephone psychics and book a reading on the numbers below:

UK: 0800 067 8600
USA: 1855 444 6887
EIRE: 1800 719 656
AUSTRALIA: 1800 825 305

Callers must be 18 or over to use this service and have the bill payers permission. For entertainment purposes only. All calls are recorded. PhonePayPlus regulated SP: StreamLive Ltd, EC4R 1BB, 0800 0673 330.

Made in the USA
San Bernardino, CA
03 December 2016